Dangerous Good is a must-read that a [barcode] worldwide injustices. By initiating cl. root issues affecting our global community, Kenny Luck is contributing to the solution. He's reaching the hearts of men and encouraging them to grow in godly character and conduct. He's reminding them that our identities are in Christ and Christ alone, and when we reflect him, we live like him—and living like him is what will change our world.

CHRISTINE CAINE, bestselling author and founder of A21 and Propel Women

I wish every Christian man—in particular every *young* man—would read and apply this book. If so, our families, churches, and relationships with nonbelievers would be transformed. Get this book, read it, and pass it off to every man you know.

SEAN MCDOWELL, PHD, Biola University professor, speaker, and author

Kenny Luck brings to light much-needed attention to a man's purpose in society. We as men must take a stand to preserve our identity in an environment that attempts to lower the bar. By giving the glory to God, Kenny shows us the path to true integrity, friendship, and the Lord's direction. The Lord has given us the directions, should we choose to follow them. By speaking to us as a man of Christ speaks to another man—as Christ spoke to his disciples—Kenny brings forth the Word of God and, in doing so, brings us closer to the Lord. Thank you, Kenny, for your leadership, dedication, and love of mankind.

MARK "OZ" GEIST, US Marine (retired), survivor of the Battle of Benghazi, as told in *13 Hours: The Secret Soldiers of Benghazi*

What I love about Kenny is that he writes in a way that gets to the heart of men. In *Dangerous Good*, he rips to the core of healthy masculinity and expresses what all men want to be true of ourselves while inviting us to use our strength for maximum impact. *Dangerous Good* is flammable, and the world wants this movement to catch fire because of the blessings it will bring to women, children, and families.

DOUG FIELDS, author and executive director, HomeWord, Azusa Pacific University

Dangerous Good is a wake-up call to all men. In this book, Kenny Luck challenges men to put down the remote control and wade into the problems in our society. Most of these problems began when good men failed to live up to the noble purpose for which God created them.

JEFF STRUECKER, author of *Bullet Proof Faith*

In *Dangerous Good*, Kenny Luck activates the hearts of men by awakening the deepest desires within them. Luck shows how easily our identities get hijacked by impostors and guides us to the dangerous-yet-good identity God desires us to find. If you want to grow in bravery or vulnerability, *Dangerous Good* will be a valuable resource for your journey.

JAY STRINGER, author of *Unwanted*

As our world grapples with what it means to be a man amidst our crumbling moral culture, Kenny Luck directs us back to the only rock-solid example—Jesus Christ. In *Dangerous Good: The Coming Revolution of Men Who Care*, Kenny explores the Bible thoroughly and thoughtfully, providing a field guide for how men can not only heal the wounds of past generations but also lead with the clarity, conviction, and compassion of Christ.

CHRIS HODGES, senior pastor at Church of the Highlands and author of *Fresh Air* and *The Daniel Dilemma*

More than a self-help book, *Dangerous Good* is a biblical play-by-play map to male authenticity and freedom in Christ. Each chapter is an intelligent and compelling guide to higher-level character, personal awareness, and a dangerously good self! Women, this is the book you've been waiting for! Toxic patriarchy and toxic feminism are turned on their heads. Christ's model of mutual respect, male integrity, and biblical feminism collaborating together for family, church, and community leads the way for a dangerously good *movement!*

ANNETTE OLTMANS, founder of The MEND Project

I love so much about this timely, inspiring book. While our culture flounders to make sense of gender differences, Kenny Luck expertly outlines the divine solution to both broken masculinity and reactive feminism, calling men to step up and into their full potential. Look out, evil: Dangerous good is coming for you!

JESSIE MINASSIAN, blogger, speaker, and author of *Family: How to Love Yours (and Help Them Like You Back)*

From the day I first met Kenny twenty-five years ago, he has always told me the truth. Nothing has changed since then. This book tells me the truth about me and the one who knows my identity best—Jesus. With memorable turns of phrase, beginning with the very title, *Dangerous Good* is a winsome, passionate, biblical call for men of God to *bear a family resemblance.*

GREG HOLDER, author of *The Genius of One*

Kenny
Luck

Dangerous
Good

The Coming
Revolution of Men
Who Care

A NavPress resource published in alliance
with Tyndale House Publishers, Inc.

NAVPRESS◯®

NavPress is the publishing ministry of The Navigators, an international Christian organization and leader in personal spiritual development. NavPress is committed to helping people grow spiritually and enjoy lives of meaning and hope through personal and group resources that are biblically rooted, culturally relevant, and highly practical.

For more information, visit www.NavPress.com.

Dangerous Good: The Coming Revolution of Men Who Care

Copyright © 2018 by Kenny Luck. All rights reserved.

A NavPress resource published in alliance with Tyndale House Publishers, Inc.

NAVPRESS and the NAVPRESS logo are registered trademarks of NavPress, The Navigators, Colorado Springs, CO. *TYNDALE* is a registered trademark of Tyndale House Publishers, Inc. Absence of ® in connection with marks of NavPress or other parties does not indicate an absence of registration of those marks.

The Team:
Don Pape, Publisher
David Zimmerman, Acquisitions Editor
Elizabeth Symm, Copy Editor
Daniel Farrell, Designer

Cover illustration of lion copyright © by Brandlogo/Creative Market. All rights reserved.

All Scripture quotations, unless otherwise indicated, are taken from the Holy Bible, *New International Version®* (*NIV®*). Copyright © 1973, 1978, 1984, 2011 by Biblica, Inc.® Used by permission. All rights reserved worldwide. Scripture quotations marked MSG are taken from *THE MESSAGE*, copyright © 1993, 1994, 1995, 1996, 2000, 2001, 2002 by Eugene H. Peterson. Used by permission of NavPress. All rights reserved. Represented by Tyndale House Publishers, Inc. Scripture quotations marked NASB are taken from the New American Standard Bible,® copyright © 1960, 1962, 1963, 1968, 1971, 1972, 1973, 1975, 1977, 1995 by The Lockman Foundation. Used by permission. Scripture quotations marked NLT are taken from the *Holy Bible*, New Living Translation, copyright © 1996, 2004, 2015 by Tyndale House Foundation. Used by permission of Tyndale House Publishers, Inc., Carol Stream, Illinois 60188. All rights reserved.

Some of the anecdotal illustrations in this book are true to life and are included with the permission of the persons involved. All other illustrations are composites of real situations, and any resemblance to people living or dead is purely coincidental.

For information about special discounts for bulk purchases, please contact Tyndale House Publishers at csresponse@tyndale.com, or call 1-800-323-9400.

Cataloging-in-Publication Data is available.

ISBN 978-1-63146-890-2

Printed in the United States of America

24 23 22 21 20 19 18
7   6   5   4   3   2   1

Dedication

Every father hopes with all his heart that the best things in him are successfully passed into and onto a son while praying that his shortcomings will be muted. But when the inner character, heart, and spiritual strength of a son comes back upon a father to bless and strengthen him, it is a gift of grace. Dangerous Good *is easily and rightfully dedicated to Ryan Luck—my son, and a brother, friend, husband, follower, and compassionate warrior. You in me, I in you, and Him in us forever.*

CONTENTS

When bad men combine, the good must
associate; else they will fall, one by one,
an unpitied sacrifice in a contemptible struggle.

EDMUND BURKE

POWERFULLY MADE

Glory—the Dangerous Good Impulse

PICTURES CAN PREDICT A PASSION.

I found an old photograph in my garage: me at four years old, sitting on a tricycle, wearing a huge Batman helmet. I paused to laugh—that helmet rarely came off my head. I was also the enthusiastic owner of Batman T-shirts, underwear, pajamas, even a toothbrush. This old, yellowing Polaroid said it all: I wanted to be Batman then.

I still want to be Batman. I am still putting down money for the movies, the apparel, the theme park experiences, the coffee mugs. Marvel and DC comics have a hold on me. And not only on me but also on men all over the world. Wherever I travel to speak, I like to ask, "How many of you owned superhero clothes or accessories when you were little?" Without fail, 90 percent of the men in the room raise their hands.

We start dreaming early. Before Batman became my thing, my dad bought me a coonskin hat, and I sang the *Davy Crockett* anthem more like a prayer than a song. When Davy Crockett lost his appeal, the coonskin cap giving way to my Batman pajamas and plastic helmet, I sang Batman's theme song—I still can. The caped crusader, too, was eventually knocked off his throne—by less mythical but equally strong men masquerading as Vikings, Steelers, and 49ers. I pestered my mom into getting me their helmets and pajamas as well. Lots of those pictures exist too.

For reasons unknown, I was drawn to men who strapped on a uniform and confronted their opposition on the way to the glory of achievement—and experienced subsequent appreciation by adoring fans. Men who faced off and showed up. As a little boy, I was searching for a way to express those very aspirations inside me. It was like I was pregnant, carrying this stuff around, looking for a way to give birth.

My guess is that you have a few pictures of your own. These vintage snapshots represent the early rumblings of a magma boiling deep within—like the steam emanating from the hillside, suggesting to a volcanologist that something's lurking underneath the ground, and soon the pressure below will overcome the pressure above.

Men and magma. It's so perfect:

- A superheated substance and force seeks a channel of expression.
- It percolates and bubbles for a long time. The passing of millennia is not unusual.
- It's energy, color, and potential—a driving force.
- When it bursts out—when the volcano erupts— it changes the landscape.
- It is rare and oddly beautiful. People want to see that bright-orange spectacle.

The aspirations we carry around in our hearts as men are like magma. They are deep inside, pushing up from within, and hoping for expression. When they surface, for better or for worse, they impact everyone.

The Eruption of a Generation

Significant volcanic eruptions are known for changing the landscape permanently. The blast zone is measured, recorded, studied, analyzed, and ranked based on the intensity and impact. The same is true for generations of men. We rise in response to the trumpet call of history to confront the issues of our time for good.

To this end, it is time for the men of *this* generation to let their aspirations inside make their way to the surface to be measured. To do so not only requires courage but also demands that this generation look at their world, look in the mirror, and then ask some deep questions. We are responsible for this hour of history—responsible before God and humanity.

Some questions a wondering world is hoping to have answered concerning this generation of men are

- What does the future of masculinity portend for humanity?
- Will masculinity continue to retain its negative connections with the world's injustices?
- Will there even be a measurable spiritual eruption of good among men in this generation?

- What aspirations do they possess that will visibly manifest?
- Will the expression feel selfish and immature or outwardly focused, for the benefit of others?
- How will women, children, and the wider society suffer or benefit?
- Will male-rooted pain keep rising in communities, or will strong love and justice rise up as it has in special generations and movements in the past?

At a precise moment in time, in a public display of identity, energy, and expression, the magma within Jesus burst forth. It came out in proclamation, then declaration, and then action. This is the ever-expanding blast of life every Christ follower has been covered and transformed by—a spiritual explosion so powerful that it is still rippling outward to the ends of the earth through willing men. The bright-orange magma shot out of Him like this:

The Spirit of the Lord is upon Me,
Because He anointed Me to preach the gospel to the poor.
He has sent Me to proclaim release to the captives,
And recovery of sight to the blind,
To set free those who are oppressed,
To proclaim the favorable year of the Lord.[1]

Jesus announced to His community that He had been *weaponized* by the Spirit of God to be dangerous with goodness. He would start crossing cultural lines and breaking the rules of broken-male culture whenever God's will or God's Word called for it.

Jesus' proclamation is ground zero of the dangerous good movement. Male culture changes over time and across cultures, but the core of it is constant: It has always been broken, just as it's always been male. Men, enticed away or wandering off from the identity given to them by God, seek a secure identity in non-gods, which then gradually take over their expression of their masculinity, which causes others to suffer.

But the same Spirit that came upon Christ, and came out of Him in words and dangerously good actions, is now at work in you. This is the direct implication for every Christ-following man—and, as we'll soon see, more significantly, for called millennial men: The Spirit is pushing up into the world, in a similar game-changing and revolutionary fashion, *through you*:

> Because you are sons, God has sent forth the Spirit of His Son into our hearts.[2]

> Those God foreknew he also predestined to be conformed to the image of his Son, that he [Christ] might be the firstborn among many brothers [us].[3]

The Spirit of the Lord is saying to the men of this generation,

> You are the brothers of the Dangerous Good One. His Spirit dwells inside of you and is seeking a

living expression through you. Every aspiration for greatness you have inside is possible, and the special power you need for your calling is standing ready to empower every act of goodness you take to the glory of God.

Sit with this. Ponder it. Receive it. Let it come over you.

Settling Is the Enemy

In any good superhero movie, the hero must overcome some force, some issue from his past, some evil, or some substance that works against his ability to protect the innocent and bring justice to the bullies. The forces working against today's generation of men on their journey toward a fulfilling and strong expression of masculinity are subtle but powerful confrontations with reality. Under the normal pressures and disappointments of life, our feelings can persuade us to lower our standards. Over time, our visions of being and doing good get hijacked or labeled unrealistic amid the swirl of life and competition on earth. Heavy gravities of existence attack our resolve, cool the magma inside, and shake us loose from our truest spiritual identity. When that happens, it starts the process we all loathe as men: *settling*.

We settle when we become content living in a way that is less than Christ's example and call upon us. We fashion a culturally safe, self-styled faith built on being not an *expression of* but *affiliated to* Jesus. We go to a worship service, we attend a small group, we read the Bible or a Christian book. We are a threat to no evil. When we are at our most timid, even the idea of a dangerous and good expression of masculinity makes us quake with fear. We don't want to appear intolerant, misogynistic, or—God forbid—masculine in a Christlike way.

Throughout history, the "masculine malaise" of identity and expression vacillates between faith and fear. This dance of identity moves men to seek inner relief and grasp at whatever assuages our male self-loathing, on the one hand, or our longing for the dangerously good expression of masculinity we lack, on the other hand. We want meaning that is uniquely masculine, but we act as though we don't know where to find it. By default, we turn to broken-male culture to define masculine meaning and promptly start borrowing trouble like schoolboys—even as Christ followers. Or worse, we blend in, play it safe, and don't rock anyone's boat.

Watching our frustration and decidedly undangerous lifestyles is the Dark One, who meets our lack of fulfillment and identity as men with lies of false greatness and glory. These lies sound good at first but ultimately hurt people or otherwise neutralize sons of the King. The message is *Be great—through indulging yourself, impressing others, increasing materially, or simply being nice.* Christ-following men might even accept a deeper deception: *Don't take your masculine identity too seriously, or people will label you as narrow-minded, intolerant, or just stupid.*

If you have any doubts about these pages from the Dark

One's playbook, dust off the Gospel of Matthew. There you'll witness the Son of God, in a weakened state, being offered false visions of greatness in a ploy to discourage Him from being dangerous with goodness.[4] Thank God Jesus didn't settle; He gave that deception a healthy whack of God's truth.

> Jesus answered, "It is written: 'Man shall not live on bread alone, but on every word that comes from the mouth of God.'"[5]

Here's the thing: We need to do the same!

Just as Jesus had this turning-point confrontation with evil, this generation of men is at its own turning point in history. A story will be told about you. It will take courage and discipline to embrace the divine hopes and aspirations connected to your life. You will have to fight to regain a foothold on the beaches of your identity, regain control of your energy, and release an expression of the character of Christ that meets your deepest needs as a man.

The first step into that fight is to become aware of a nasty and intentional cultural campaign that has been messing with your identity and destiny as a Christ follower. The second step is to realize that the truest thing about you is what God says is true. His message to the brothers of Jesus? You are His, and eternity is coming.

Deep within you is a voice you have been trying to compartmentalize, rationalize, mute, or simply explain. In your heart, you know that you are more than what you have become, and you can't become the man you were created to be by remaining who you are. The answer to this dilemma is near, not far: Christ in you. With that in mind and looking ahead to the rest of the dangerous good journey we'll explore in this book, I have only one encouragement: Don't dabble.

Eternity Calling

In the Bible, Solomon dabbled with his identity, compartmentalized his calling, and experimented with identities outside of God. He reflected on his journey—the inner conflicts and the struggle to find spiritual clarity and masculine success—in the book of Ecclesiastes. There we find him paralyzed by seeing the answer and the problem at the same time:

> He has planted eternity in the human heart, but
> even so, people cannot see the whole scope of God's
> work from beginning to end.[6]

He had the problem right intellectually, but he was trapped in the fog of his own hesitations and bad choices. He had to fight to see clearly. This was a man of God who guzzled at the fountain of cultural masculinity. Plenty of pleasure. Plenty of power. Plenty of possessions. And puh-lenty of women. But now, with the clarity only hindsight can give, he grieved his life and lamented over selecting the wrong vision for finding meaning as a man. In this way, he speaks for hundreds of millions of men who sense the same dilemma.

As God's Spirit moves upon and quickens the hearts of this generation of Christ-following men, whole communities of guys all over the world are reconnecting masculinity to eternity. The strong, transcendent purpose of Jesus Christ is being released for this time in history, and it is flooding into the hearts of willing men seeking a dangerous good identity right now.

There's only one realm in which the dangerous good impulse becomes a life-giving reality: the Kingdom of God. It has a King, it has authority, and it has an experience we can enter into as men without wishing, fantasizing, hoping, or wearing a superhero suit.

The ever-growing movement emanating out of the Kingdom of God will be increasingly visible and distinct in all human history with respect to its intentions and actions. It will deliver masculinity out of its cultural labels, caricatures, and quagmires of disrespect and doubt into the shining light of Christ. Most importantly, it will enter the small spaces where life is really felt, redeeming them and bringing to them Kingdom power, life-giving help, justice, and compassion.

The world has been waiting for this movement for a long time. Evil has been fearing it, and Jesus has been planning His return around it.

It's what we have felt and wanted since we were four years old in our Batman helmets.

The Dangerous Good are coming.

01

POWERFULLY FORMED MEN

Identity—the Lost Lions

You don't even know who you are! . . . You're Mufasa's boy.

RAFIKI TO SIMBA, *THE LION KING*

SIMBA IS A "LOST" LION.

If you haven't seen the Disney film about a lion who has lost track of who he really is, go find it, stream it, download it, whatever—and watch it. Simba is a lion cub, the son of the king: a clear bloodline, a clear connection to a clear destiny. At some future moment, he *will* take his father's place. But as life unfolds for the lion cub, events disrupt his smooth transition to the top. He panics and runs (literally) from his identity, responsibility, and destiny into a world that takes the pressure off.

Simba is not lost *directionally.* He actually knows where he is. But he has "lost his way" in terms of his identity. That's what makes this story so sad and so powerful at the same time. Lions are majestic. Lions belong to prides. Lions—especially the male ones—lead. But Simba grows into a young male lion separated from his pride.

The world Simba has built for himself eventually collides with reality: His pride—his kingdom—is suffering in the absence of a good leader. Simba starts receiving some direct messages that his pride needs him badly. Enter Rafiki the baboon, and Simba's reckoning.

Simba tries to run from Rafiki and his challenge, but "You're Mufasa's boy" means the game is up. Simba is out of place, not doing what he's supposed to be doing. It's a grabbing by the ear, a kick in the backside, and a confrontation of his true identity. Hanging in the air are basic questions: Why are you here? What are you doing? Have you forgotten who you are?

The Lion King is a parable in the tradition of Jesus' parables, which ominously and accurately confront people where they are with who they are. It is particularly significant for this time in history—especially for Millennial men who identify with and follow Jesus Christ. Tens of millions of "Simbas" worldwide—sons of the King in the prime of their lives—are being confronted by the Spirit of God, reminded who they truly are, what the true need of the Kingdom is right now, and what the truest purposes are for a son of the King. Out-of-place sons of God are being chased down, and the Holy Spirit is saying, *I know who you really are. The*

Kingdom calls. Lives are at stake, evil must be confronted, and you are the one who's going to do it.

It's an exciting time as God gathers His own for a showdown with evil.

It's a risk-filled and faith-stretching time of loving confrontation over our identity.

It's time to take your place.

Leaving the "Bubble"

As the story of Simba vividly illustrates, sometimes even those of us who think we know who we are (or who have been told who we are our whole lives by our culture, our family of origin, or God Himself) wander and need reminding. This is a prodigal journey, and it takes many forms—some you would never expect. Maybe college knocked you off the path your identity calls you to. Or perhaps you mistakenly felt you had to be your own man and make your own way, and the faith of your family didn't allow for that, so you caved.

Many men have chosen a Christ-free identity because they were attacked by their own—injured by some well-meaning but insecure Christians who made them feel as though they weren't Christian enough.

For others, innocent wandering turned into a sprint away from your truest identity and toward the world—you knew being a "Jesus guy" meant not winning the approval of others, which, at the time, meant more to you than God's approval.

Regardless of form, prodigal journeys always start with

high hopes for the better. But the idealized version of life outside of Christ eventually bursts like a bubble, leading to prodigal pain.

It's a bittersweet moment. The bitter is all the negative emotions that come with pain. The sweet is that with the "bubble" gone, you can return home to Jesus, who is eagerly waiting for you.

If you are reading this and thinking, *That's not me and it never was*, don't get too smug. Many modern-day Simbas haven't run, but they are most definitely playing it safe in the comfortable ranks of the pride. These are sons of the King— they grew up in the faith. Maybe they were dedicated to God as babies. They attended church and went to Christian camp every summer. They have multiple Bibles and smokin' playlists on their phones right now that exalt Jesus. They may even sport a spiritually inspired tattoo, maybe a Greek word that communicates *Jesus, love, grace, forgiven, the cross*, or *commitment*. These sons may be young marrieds with kids, good guys, providers. They take their families to church most Sundays, would never cheat on their women, and have a better relationship with their kids than their dad had with them. If you asked them if they love Jesus, their answer would be an unequivocal "Yes, I do" or "I am a Christ follower."

Are they affiliated to Jesus? Yes. Are they activated for Jesus? No.

Are they good guys? Yes. Are they dangerous good? No.

Do they resist evil? Yes. Do they pose a threat to evil? Not even on the devil's radar.

Unchallenged, they remain holy bubble boys, and "It's all good, bro." It doesn't require real faith to keep up the bubble-boy lifestyle, and whatever that lifestyle is, it is not *holy*. It is, rather, *safe*. But God is intentionally bursting their bubbles.

Your bubble might just have popped right now.

God's holding for you on Line 1.

I Want My Sons Back

This is not the first generation of God's sons to wander and be called back to their truest identity. The prophetic words of Jeremiah travel hauntingly through time amid today's generation:

> Thus says the LORD to the men of Judah and to Jerusalem,

> "Break up your fallow ground,
> and do not sow among thorns.
> Circumcise yourselves to the LORD
> And remove the foreskins of your heart."[1]

Ouch. The unmistakable and convicting message from God to His sons? "Come out of culture, come back to covenant, and start being fruitful and productive for my purposes. Do whatever you have to do, inside or out, and do it now."

In Jeremiah's generation, most guys were farmers. They knew what God meant when He told them to stop wasting their energy sowing among thorns. He was telling them not to give the best days of their best years to a fruitless, godless culture. They also knew that in order to answer God's call, they were going to have to pay a price. Breaking up, reworking, and refertilizing the abandoned or unplowed ground of their relationship with God was going to be painful—it would produce some spiritual sweat and require real work—but it would be worth it.

And then the spiritual thoracic saw came out: Their chests were going to be cracked open for a self-administered open-heart surgery.

Picture that for a second. Gnarly, isn't it?

Why surgery? Because God wanted to save their hearts, hearts that had been infected and diseased by the idols of the age, and refashion them around their identity in God, setting them apart once again for God's purposes. There is no chance these sons of Covenant could miss God's point.

Now it's your turn. This is a prophetic word for this generation's sons of the King.

God wants His sons back—all of them, especially those who have wandered off or feel cast out. He doesn't want *affiliated* sons; He wants *activated* sons who are dangerous with goodness like Christ and who understand they have limited time and a scheduled meeting when their heart stops. He wants sons who know they are created by God, created for God, and going back to God, and who use that awareness to discipline their energy toward Kingdom purposes. He wants sons who think like His Son, who find satisfaction in what satisfies Him: "My food," Jesus says, "is to do the will of him who sent me and to finish his work."[2]

The King is calling a generation of sons to bear the family resemblance, understand the urgency of the hour, and act in awareness that tomorrow is not guaranteed. The Spirit is calling out around the world to the sons of the King—and saying to you directly—that while not all who have wandered are lost, there comes a time when wandering must end and transform into purposeful pilgrimage.

God's Spirit is welling up in you for a reason: The King has summoned you back; He is requiring a full surrender to His kingship and Kingdom call.

Practically, that means you need to take to heart that you are not a son of culture, you are a son of Christ. It's time to aggressively activate your identity. What's the alternative? Remain an affiliated follower, which is a follower in name only.

The Holy Spirit knows who you are. Do you?

The question of identity is issue number one to God because whatever commands your identity will, by default, command your energy—either toward or away from God's dangerous good agenda for your life. Every core identity outside of our core identity in Christ saps a man's energy. A materialist at the core dedicates his energy to making bank and accumulating stuff. A hedonist at his core puts all his time, thoughts, and dollars into self-gratifying pursuits. A narcissist at his core spends massive amounts of his energy on elevating his own visibility, at whatever human or financial cost. All the identities the world has to offer make gods out of things that are not gods, and these non-gods creep into the lives of God's sons, polluting their identity and diluting their energy for God.

The Bible suggests that a yes to Jesus is, by default, a no to other identities.

Watch your identity carefully: It will command your energy and should lead you to a dangerous good expression as a son of Christ.

But you, man of God, flee from all this, and pursue righteousness, godliness, faith, love, endurance and gentleness. Fight the good fight of the faith. Take hold of the eternal life to which you were called when you made your good confession in the presence of many witnesses.[3]

Just prior to this charge to Timothy, Paul offered a clear rejection of the materialist identity. Instead, Timothy is called "man of God," an identity with implications for where to go and not go, what to say yes and no to, and, above all, where to put big energy in order to produce a strong eternal expression.

The point here is sharp: *The man of God is not a spectator to God's Kingdom purposes being advanced on earth.* God never intended His sons to *watch* the battle between evil and good; He expects us to *fight* for the good of our faith—in the open, living out the dangerous good calling we have in Him, and, in the process, restating our identity in Christ to the world!

Notice that the dangerous good call each other by their real name: man of God. We speak the man-of-God identity into the chests of our brothers to remind them of their identity. It's one of the best and most powerful things we can do: drive the truest thing about a man deeper into his spirit, deeper into his thinking, and deeper into his living. The great apostle knew identity was the secret power that would (and still does) drive the next generation of Timothys to rise up. He would speak it over them, and they would accept it as the final determiner of who they would be, what they would believe, and how they would behave in their generation.

That's what this conversation right now is all about: a laser-guided reminder that you are His. As the dangerous good, it is our duty to remind one another:

> I will always be ready to remind you of these
> things, even though you already know them,
> and have been established in the truth which is
> present with you. I consider it right, as long as
> I am in this earthly dwelling, to stir you up by
> way of reminder.[4]

The Truest Thing about You

The truest thing about you is what God says is true.

Competing voices and forces are in a recruiting war over whose version of yourself you will accept, internalize, believe, and then put your energy behind. But when the man of God believes and acts upon what *God* says is true about him, an explosion of personal transformation occurs.

You abandon any image of yourself that is not from God.

You stop chasing, caring about, and accepting what others say about you.

You're not defined by your feelings.

You are not defined by your circumstances.

You are not defined by your successes or failures.

You are not defined by the car you drive, the money you make, or the house you say you own (the bank owns it, actually).

You are defined—and redefined—by God and God alone (see Colossians 3:10).

In its purest essence, the dangerous good revolution is a revolution of your perspective on you!

But why? Why should I let God redefine me? Why should I release every last part of my will to this process? What will God do in my life if I say yes? If you are not asking these kinds of questions, you should. If I were being asked to accelerate my spiritual commitment to the level of "dangerous good," I would want to know what I was getting into. What can I expect in real time and in my real life?

Fortunately, we have a complete picture available to us of what a dangerous good life looks like. Jesus came and lived His life as a man; as such, we have a model in real time for how a man lives out his truest identity. He came not only to show us that living for an audience of one is the right way to be, believe, and behave, but also to motivate us to do the same as men in our time and context. Masculinity starts and stops with Jesus. He is both alpha and omega male when it comes to living in front of God.

Jesus not only shows us what the dangerous good identity *looks* like but also helps us understand what being a man should *feel* like. That's right—I just connected the words *feel* and *man*. Not to worry though, because what we see happening in Christ defies the gender-bending labels of today's culture, transcending and overcoming them. Jesus brings masculinity to a place where cultural man cannot go but where every man on planet earth longs to be: a place where danger and good come together.

As you see Jesus, see yourself reproducing His life in your context. This "identity-driven life" is your precise answer to how a man of God lives, what it means, and how it feels in the masculine context. Specifically, Jesus shows you four things.

Living Out My Truest Identity Gives Me the Greatest Integrity

> They came to him and said, "Teacher, we know
> that you are a man of integrity. You aren't swayed by
> others, because you pay no attention to who they
> are; but you teach the way of God in accordance
> with the truth."[5]

The word *integrity* comes from the math term *integer*, which means whole or undivided. To possess personal and spiritual integrity means to have a life that is undivided between what you believe and how you actually live and think in real time. Jesus knew that He came from God and that He was going back to God; He knew who He was, so He didn't have to become someone else. His identity in the Father provided an uncommon power over the opinions of people regarding His behavior, as well as an uncommon ability to advance God's purposes without worry. His critics could not accuse Him of hypocrisy; even though they wanted to find dirt, Jesus was the real deal and they had to admit it.

Jesus was not a man pleaser but a God pleaser. He was an audience-of-one kind of guy. He didn't have to overthink social settings or situational ethics because His identity told Him to do that one thing that would show love for God and people in a given moment.

That meant Jesus broke the rules of broken-male culture when compassion or God's Word required it. That is significant. The religious men of Jesus' day marginalized women, children, and Gentiles (non-Jews). As we can see, Jesus wasn't swayed by those men. There is your working definition of integrity and the by-product of a true identity in God: God's man does not pander to people, but lives out God's purposes regardless of the rules of culture. He is a son of Christ, not a son of culture.

The dangerous good revolution is marked by spiritual integrity and will be a movement of *fearless men who are like Jesus.*

Living Out My Truest Identity Gives Me My Strongest Liberty

[Jesus said,] "The Son of Man came eating and drinking, and they say, 'Here is a glutton and a drunkard, a friend of tax collectors and sinners.' But wisdom is proved right by her deeds."[6]

Unbound by the opinions of men and only concerned about the opinion of the Father, Jesus was free to associate with anyone and care for anyone. In fact, His identity in the Father provided Him with such a transcendent freedom that people mistook it for having low standards.

When we watch Jesus live out His truest identity, we both see and sense a personal liberty of thought and action. We see Jesus regularly accept those deemed physically unacceptable (lepers), ethnically unacceptable (Samaritans), morally unacceptable (prostitutes), and socially unacceptable (tax collectors) into His life and ministry. His identity in the Father allowed Him to jettison the boundaries and self-absorption of broken-male culture and get into the lives of those who most needed the grace and truth of God.

There is your working definition of personal liberty and the by-product of a true identity in God: God's man is set free to care about, serve, and dignify people whom lesser men abuse, exploit, or marginalize. He is a son of Christ, not a son of culture.

The dangerous good revolution will be a movement of *free men who are like Jesus.*

Living Out My Truest Identity Gets My Best Energy

> [Jesus said,] "As long as it is day, we must do the
> works of him who sent me. Night is coming,
> when no one can work."[7]

A fireman puts out fires. A policeman protects the community against lawbreakers. A businessman makes money by providing a service. A foreman manages a project through to completion. What does a man of God do?

Again, our precise example is Jesus. The Son of God does the works of God He has been put on earth to do. The man of God imitates the Son of God and focuses his heart, soul, mind, and strength on doing the works of God with Jesus.

Jesus did not dabble around.

Three years, twelve men, and ultimately twenty centuries of movement were the result of an extremely strong identity and a correspondingly strong focus in His earthly years. Jesus knew the clock was ticking, and such knowledge creates urgency. Urgency, in turn, creates energy and intentionality of effort.

The picture Jesus paints for His followers above is that of a window of time closing on us. Think about an elevator you need to get on and the doors are starting to close. What do you do? Think about the game clock when your team is behind in a close game. How are they acting on the court or field? Think about a surfer who sees the wave he's been waiting for all morning suddenly start to build on the ocean horizon. How does he react?

Jesus' identity as Son of the Father drove His perspective. He was on mission to accomplish what God had uniquely given Him to do during His limited time on earth. The key word? *Limited.* He did not get bogged down in peripheral, trivial, or temporal focuses competing for His energy. He chose instead to focus on what was central to His identity: heaven.

Specifically, we see the Son of God telling people how to get to heaven, blessing others in ways that helped them to recognize the God of heaven, and completing His mission on earth in anticipation of His return to heaven. There is your working definition of giving your best energy as the by-product of a true identity in God: God's man is on mission in his context—in his geographical space, in his spheres of influence, with the people and opportunities God has given him. He knows intuitively that he has limited time, an unknown ending, and a scheduled meeting with Jesus Himself. He is focused on hearing at that meeting, "Well done, good and faithful servant!"[8] He is a son of Christ, not a son of culture.

The dangerous good revolution will be a movement of *focused men who are like Jesus.*

My Truest Identity Reflects My Ultimate Destiny

Jesus . . . looked toward heaven and prayed: "Father, the hour has come. Glorify your Son, that your Son may glorify you. For you granted him authority over all people that he might give eternal life to all those you have given him. Now this is eternal life: that they know you, the only true God, and Jesus Christ, whom you have sent. I have brought you glory on earth by finishing the work you gave me to do. And now, Father, glorify me in your presence with the glory I had with you before the world began.[9]

What happens when we die? How you answer that question directly reflects your identity. A man of God believes he's going to God, and when he goes, it's not for the purpose of being ruled in or out of heaven but to be examined as a manager of his life.

Before Jesus went voluntarily to the cross, He contemplated His physical death, offering His most transparent and reflective prayers. Some personal accounting with respect to His life's journey was taking place in this prayer.

The prayer process revealed the thinking process: *Let's see. Did I bring God glory? Check. Did I do on earth what God put me here to do? Check. Can I return home with a clear conscience that I did everything I could to reveal God's love and plan? Check.*

Jesus' prayer reveals that He was ready to go back home to the Father: He had no unfinished business here on earth; He had been faithful; He was complete. His prayer functioned as a kind of final check with the Father.

There is your working definition of how your truest identity reflects your ultimate destiny: God's man knows that his identity in the Father includes being with the Father forever. The visible fruit of that knowledge is faithfulness to the end and completeness when the end comes—no unfinished business.

The dangerous good revolution will be a movement of *faithful men who are like Jesus.*

Passing the Torch

Living out your truest identity in God is the essence of true masculinity.

Don't let rip-off ways of being, believing, and behaving rob you of becoming the dangerous good man God created you to be. I will say it again: You are a son of Christ, not a son of culture.

Examine yourself and know that God wants His sons at full force. Secure in our truest identity and with the Spirit of Christ inside us, we will know what it means to live fearless, free, focused, and faithful to the Father's ultimate purpose and destiny for us.

Only when we know what is true about ourselves and our specific purpose can we actually pull that off. Knowing that I am made by God, for God's works, and I am going back to God should change everything. *But will it?*

Jesus is commissioning you and me to live out our truest identity in the Father *in our time*:

> Very truly I tell you, whoever believes in me will do
> the works I have been doing, and they will do even
> greater things than these, because I am going to
> the Father.[10]

Read that passage again and let those words grip your spirit. Let the prophetic declaration over you sink into your soul. Let the expectation of Christ create a healthy and holy fear. Let the reality of your life to this point encourage you or convict you or both. Let it happen.

This is the truest direction you can receive in this moment. God is speaking, and He is executing a good old-fashioned hand-off: "Whoever believes in me will do the works I have been doing." Key words? *Will do.* Don't debate it. Don't deny it. Don't deflect it. Say yes to your identity in Christ, and put your energy where God has said it is supposed to go— immediately. Be a man by being like the Son of Man while there is still time. You may have wandered, but you are not a lost lion any more. You have been reminded. The Spirit knows who you are: You are the son of the King. The reckoning is now because the revolution is about to begin.

Dangerous Good Conversation

What is the truest thing about you?

Reflect on times you have run away from that identity. Why did you run?

What motivates you the most: Integrity? Liberty? Energy? Destiny? Why?

How have you experienced these benefits of finding your identity in Christ alone?

02

POWERFULLY CONVICTED MEN

Morality—Simple but Strong

——

Tolerance is the virtue of the man without convictions.

G. K. CHESTERTON

CHRISTOPHER LANE'S LIFE WAS ANYTHING BUT BORING.

He was a college athlete and leader. He had met a wonderful girl in Duncan, Oklahoma, a small town of around twenty-four thousand. While visiting her one day, Christopher decided to go for a jog. You could be him right now.

His only mistake? Running on the sidewalk past a home filled with young men without any moral convictions or conscience. One young man saw Christopher jog by and said to the others, "There's our target." They piled into a car and proceeded to follow him. Then they shot him in the back. He staggered for a few feet and collapsed as they drove off.

The young man who shot Lane told police, "We were

bored and didn't have anything to do, so we decided to kill somebody."[1] The motive? *For the fun of it.*

Think about that for a second. It's called living in a moral vacuum.

Morally untrained young men have been to policemen what "unaccounted for" uranium represents to counterterrorism worldwide: a threat to peace, to innocent people— a major problem that demands attention because young men's potential can easily be "weaponized." All it takes is *a really bad idea* offered in the absence of moral training and convictions. Into the vacuum will come a voice, a neuron fires, and words are expressed that are terrifying. "I got it!" he says to himself. "Wouldn't it be cool if . . . we killed someone?" The company of men ratify the idea; it is welcomed and executed without filters and without objection. In their minds, they are actually energized and thinking, *This is gonna be* fun.

The excitement rising from such a deadly brainstorm is not just about a lazy summer, it's about *attempting to become men* in a cesspool of self-serving convictions that exploit a man's natural quest for acceptance and worth. Peer opinion, male angst, and self-loathing are the drivers instead of higher purposes, compassionate concern, and moral accountability to God and your fellow man. The result: a dangerous male culture that trains young men to act selfishly and to separate their hearts from their heads when a decision they make impacts others negatively. It's called *alexithymia.* Look it up. The roots that form the word mean "to repel the soul." It is a picture of being emotionally dead or without the ability to feel empathy for another person.

Culture today is creating these types of young men by the millions. They will in turn produce multiplied billions of real social interactions, creating a titanic wave of injustice and trauma for themselves and scores of innocent people. Emotionally unaware and socially detached, these young men cannot connect their actions with the feelings of others. This type of male compartmentalization provides the inner freedom and sanction necessary to kill, make others suffer, and then *talk about it objectively*, like the young men in this case. The police interviews with the young men in the Christopher Lane story are surreal. They talk about killing a man the way a person would describe building a roast beef sandwich. It's on the level of "We were hungry, so we ate." And they did it together! In the end, their behaviors reflected their beliefs.

Every man has a mental marinade of thoughts that flavors all our actions. We get to choose the ingredients. Some men soak their minds in sports news; you find them regularly catching up on the weekend's game results, lamenting the underperformance of their fantasy team, or watching highlights on a sports app. Other men choose to soak their minds in sexual thoughts and porn, which leads to sexual acting out in private or public. Some men are constantly trolling online, eyeballing their next big purchase. Still other men soak their minds in Scripture, seeking after what God thinks and letting it inform their perceptions of life and people. You will find these men reading books like the one you are holding, pondering what it means for them, and taking action for Christ. Whatever their nature, the things we think about marinate in our minds, coalescing into beliefs and values that shape behaviors that bring harm or health to our connections to God and people.

That powerful fact that beliefs and behaviors are connected spotlights the real convictions of the current generation of God's men and how they are living their own beliefs out in the open *together*—or not. The men who took Christopher Lane's life banded together in a vacuum of morality. What about those among us who possess the Spirit of Christ? When we watch tragedies like this unfold, our blood boils and our spirits are appalled, but many times we fail to ask the bigger questions like

- Where are the men of this generation who believe their beliefs as aggressively as this group of men— but for God and good?
- Where are they banding together?
- What activities and investment of energy are bonding them and making news?
- Where is the visible intersection of strong men and strong morality to welcome the next generation who are falling through the cracks and into the dark moral vacuum?

For any man of God, shining the light of Christ in his generation implies that he does it in front of people so that others can plainly see him, be drawn to the light of God in him, and find hope and help in the process. When communities of God's men shine the light of Christ, that effect is multiplied, accelerated, and seen around the world because it is so rare. Against the backdrop of the chaos, dysfunction, and seemingly hopeless state of broken masculinity are the dazzling diamonds of Jesus—His men. The world is waiting for this light show of real men with real convictions who bring real hope by their very presence:

> You are the light of the world. A town built on a hill cannot be hidden. Neither do people light a lamp and put it under a bowl. Instead they put it on its stand, and it gives light to everyone in the house. In the same way, let your light shine before others, that they may see your good deeds and glorify your Father in heaven.[2]

Only one thing left to do now: Start shining.

The Light of Believing Your Beliefs

Exercising spiritual confidence through openly living out your convictions always benefits you and others, but Someone particularly is watching with a keen eye, hopeful heart, and strong expectation.

God.

"My righteous one will live by faith.
And I take no pleasure
in the one who shrinks back."

But we do not belong to those who shrink back
and are destroyed, but to those who have faith and
are saved."[3]

I don't blame you if you read that again. God's forceful position on your faith expression is both challenging and motivating, depending on your perspective. On the one side, His heart is beating with eager anticipation over a moment in time when His sons have their chance to exercise world-changing faith. He is a confident and proud Father who has given us a charge and mission that is fully supported by His person and power. He knows who He is and what He can do, and He has placed all that power at our disposal. He also knows that whatever fear or obstacle is before us, it will never be bigger than His person, who is standing behind us right now. Those are the facts, whether or not we are in touch with them at any given moment.

When men who declare faith in Him retreat spiritually, God is offended, because it sends the message that the God we serve is either unable to honor His Word, unwise in His directions, or unloving in His purposes. Shrinking back when you have superiority of power and a plan to redeem every action taken in His name simply doesn't make sense. That's why He can say, "I take no pleasure in the one who shrinks back." It's not about you, it's about what your behavior among men says about Him. A man with a clear vision of God may delay obedience temporarily, but he is inevitably drawn back to the chance to trust God's promise.

Seeing God's perspective gives us a little insight into why David was the man who won over God's heart in his generation.

> God testified concerning him: "I have found David son of Jesse, a man after my own heart; he will do everything I want him to do."[4]

The key for David, for you, and for every man of God walking planet earth right now is that we decide to do whatever God asks *in advance* of Him asking! That's the secret to possessing powerful convictions and winning each moment for Christ. When your convictions are clear, your decisions are easy, your impact increases, and you develop a godly consistency—all from simply deciding *right now* that you will do what God wants when the moment comes, whatever that moment looks like. You make the decision when your head is clear and life is free from that pressure.

But make no mistake: The pressure of the moment is on its way! What happens to the man who doesn't have a right view of God, whose identity is not settled, and who has not decided in advance to do what God wants him to do? Jesus' half-brother James clearly knew men in both camps and had this to say:

The one who doubts is like a wave of the sea, blown
and tossed by the wind. That person should not
expect to receive anything from the Lord. Such a
person is double-minded and unstable in all they do.[5]

Doubting God leads to inconsistency in your commitment
to Christ based on convenience and comfort. God simply cannot bless such vacillation. Do you blame Him? When a man
makes a vow to his wife at the altar, God asks for a commitment in advance: Each person pledges to be faithful regardless
of circumstances. Never in a ceremony has a groom responded
to my question with "I will . . . *most of the time.*" That response
would be greeted by his bride with first confusion, then distance, and ultimately, separation. Similarly, a lack of confidence *in God* reflects itself in equally weak convictions *for God*,
resulting in a lack of power and blessing *from God*. But if you
take what God says in His Word and turn it upside down, an
equally powerful picture and motivation comes into play: The
one who is confident in God, single-minded, and stable in
what he does should expect to receive all of what God promises. Such is a man of conviction.

Specifically, God will bless and use your strong convictions to better

- *Defuse conflict.* When your values and beliefs are clear,
  your decision-making process becomes significantly
  easier and less stressful. True convictions eliminate most
  conflicts before they even arise. But if you want higher

levels of stress and conflict, weak convictions about moral and relational issues will help.

- *Defeat temptation.* Only strong convictions have the power to defeat strong temptations in real time. In Luke 4, we see this scenario when Jesus is tempted. A strong temptation is slam-dunked verbally by a strong conviction from God's Word. What Jesus models for us is meant for us.

- *Direct others.* The best advisers have the clarity of their convictions and real-life experiences from relying on them to back up their counsel. When you ask a person with weak convictions "What do you think I should do?" they will tell you to do what you feel is best. Thanks a lot.

- *Deliver help.* How do I know when I'm supposed to stop what I'm doing to help another person? When should I get involved or insert myself into a situation? Your response will be based either on your convictions or on your convenience. One filter serves others. The other serves only you.

- *Discern right and wrong.* Self or others? Compete or connect? Serve or be served? Your strong spiritual convictions answer all these questions clearly and forcefully and will call you forward in Christ.

Weak convictions for God and His purposes help nobody, but strong convictions help everybody—especially other men who are on the fence and watching you live your life. That's why the dangerous good movement in today's world is so explosive. There are millions of guys straddling the fence of their spiritual commitment to Jesus; all it's going to take is the wind of your life to blow on another man's flickering ember of commitment to bring its potential into another real flame. That process will then repeat itself all over the world until heaven lights up every true son of God.

Convictions will be the kindling. Belief will be the spark. Faith and trust in the moment will be the wildfire that turns the horizon reddish orange in a worldwide movement of God's Spirit.

Simple Convictions, Many Expressions

Having strong convictions and shining the light of Christ simply means to be persuaded—free of doubt—about the most important things. It does not mean never doubting. It does not require Bible expertise. Nor does it mean you drop all your friends and go monastic. Listen to, study, and watch Jesus—the most strongly convicted but approachable man ever to walk the planet. He is our model for the dangerous good movement, as well as our mentor. He stood out and so will we.

Curious about His theology, men peppered Jesus with questions designed to put Him into one of their boxes. That way, as in modern politics today, they could label Him, discredit Him, and consolidate their own followings. It was clear to His critics (and there were plenty) He was a strong leader, but there was something different about the way He worked out His belief in God so seamlessly among varying groups of people. He floated freely between the Temple, the market, and the countryside. He was winning over the highly religious as well as the smelly ragamuffins, but He did not demand that people obsess over a big list of dos and don'ts.

Finally, in what turned out to be part ambush and part inquisition, the exasperated religious men cornered Jesus and forced Him to put a theological stake in the ground. They wanted Jesus to answer the question every seeker of God wants to know: "What do I need to do in order to please God, go to heaven, and experience His true purpose here on earth, right now?"

What followed is the greatest spiritual statement of all time. Let's roll the film.

> One of them, an expert in the law, tested him with this question: "Teacher, which is the greatest commandment in the Law?"
>
> Jesus replied: "'Love the Lord your God with all your heart and with all your soul and with all your mind.' This is the first and greatest commandment. And the second is like it: 'Love your neighbor as yourself.' All the Law and the Prophets hang on these two commandments."[6]

Based on their reaction, Jesus' answer was overwhelmingly brilliant and stunningly simple. The model, mentor, and messenger of this new wave of spirituality and masculinity said that His followers need to possess two simple convictions. When in doubt, Jesus declared, do these things wherever you are, whoever you are with, in whatever situation you find yourself: Show love for God and love for people. Hold to those simple convictions and you will be good with God, good with people, and a brightly shining light for Christ in a dark world.

The secret sauce of life with God—the secret to doing the right thing 100 percent of the time—came down to making a commitment to God and a commitment to other people. No more ten commandments. No more long lists. No more anxiety or overthinking. No more should I or shouldn't I? Just do what shows love for God and love for people. We can *all* do that.

Loving God, Jesus emphasized, simply means doing what pleases God:

Whoever has my commands and keeps them is the one who loves me. The one who loves me will be loved by my Father, and I too will love them and show myself to them.[7]

The one who sent me is with me; he has not left me alone, for I always do what pleases him.[8]

Good news for the dangerous good: *You don't have to overanalyze or overthink anything.* You simply need to ask: What does God think about this? What does He say about it? Then do that in faith, trusting that God knows best how to manage life and relationships. Learning His Word and doing what He says is "keeping His commands" and sends the most direct and powerful message to God that you love Him. There is no substitute in Jesus' mind. That's it. It also sends a message to everyone connected to you that you are committed to loving God. Lots of men have beliefs *about God* but the dangerous good man *lives them out* in the open and, in the process, turns them into convictions. The ember of commitment turns into a flame.

The other big wheel, Jesus said, turns on a very simple axle:

Do to others as you would have them do to you.
  If you love those who love you, what credit is that to you? Even sinners love those who love them.[9]

In Matthew's Gospel (and then recast in Luke's Gospel in response to a different topic), Jesus offers the greatest piece of relational advice ever given. In doing so, He kills two birds with one stone: He gives us a command to keep and turn into a conviction that we can take into virtually any relationship, and, at the same time, He forces us to confront our selfish double standard. Friendships, marriages, families, workplaces, neighborhoods, communities, countries, and whole cultures across the centuries have been the beneficiaries of this small axle of conviction turning the big wheel of loving people just the right way. Both parties are blessed, God is glorified, and, more important, the light of Christ is shining for all to see. It's called the *principle of reciprocity*, and you can't have relationships without it.

Again, more good news for the dangerous good: To live out this conviction, all one must do is ask, "How would I want someone to deal with me in the same situation?" If you run into a wall trying to pull that off in your relationships, we have what is called the "one another's" in God's Word: commands that encompass forgiving, encouraging, loving, and serving one another.

Sometimes I wish there were a pill I could take that would guarantee unselfish and loving responses to all the people in my life at all times. Wake up, take the pill, love others well, go to sleep, and repeat the process. Unfortunately, it's not that simple. If I don't get enough sleep or feel lonely in the midst of life, I can get sour with others. If I skip a meal, the whole enchilada can come tumbling down! Then other times, it's just the brokenness of earth and my circumstances becoming too much that turns me into an emotional porcupine! Very hard to love. But that's when I am reminded that in order to love my neighbor as myself, I have to focus on my first priority: loving God. They are connected. The more I am loving God—spending time with Him, talking to Him, giving things over to Him, and listening intently to what He says—the more loving I tend to be. I try to heed Jesus' advice to keep it simple and keep it strong.

As we think about our world right now, one thing is for sure: We need all men who bear Christ's name to possess these two simple convictions and live them out aggressively in the big and small spaces of their lives. With between six hundred and seven hundred million Christ-following men alive on planet earth in this hour of history, the resulting choices based on these two simple and strong convictions would mean billions of Christlike expressions worldwide. Evil would take a hit at every level of society, in every community, and in every country. Tens of millions would be blessed; millions of people would see Jesus Christ in us and believe in Him for the first time. It's time to manifest what the Swiss theologian Karl Barth called the "New Testament power of spiritual aggression."[10] That is, simple convictions aggressively lived out.

Possessing and forcefully living out these two simple convictions uncomplicates the spiritual life and, at the same time, activates an avalanche of good. That event will hinge on you making a strong choice to fight for them in your life. It's called the "good fight" in Scripture.

> Fight the good fight of the faith. Take hold of the
> eternal life to which you were called when you
> made your good confession in the presence of many
> witnesses.[11]

If you want to be free in this fight, hold aggressively to your morality—which looks like loving God and loving people. If you want to eliminate distractions to your spiritual walk, do the same. Eliminate your detractors' influence over your decisions? Same. Eliminate doubt in your spirit? Same. Your strong convictions going forward will make you free in the fight, just like Jesus—free to live for God and love others in an attractive and powerful way.

> [Jesus said,] "The student is not above the teacher, but everyone who is fully trained will be like their teacher."[12]

Keep it simple, but keep it strong.

Dangerous Good Conversation

Where have you observed the weaponization of young men's potential—the toxic combination of a moral vacuum and a bad idea?

Which of the following motivates you the most to strengthen your convictions and commitments: Defusing conflict? Defeating temptation? Directing others? Delivering help? Discerning right from wrong? Why?

Jesus boils conviction down to two commitments: loving God and loving neighbors. What causes you to overcomplicate conviction? How has the Great Commandment simplified your commitments?

03

POWERFULLY CONNECTED MEN

Community—the Spirit of the Rapscallion

Real spiritual friendship is eagerly helping one another know,
serve, love, and resemble God in deeper and deeper ways.

TIMOTHY KELLER

"MRS. LUCK, CAN KENNY COME OUT AND PLAY?"

The two rapscallions standing on my porch looking quizzically up at my mom were loved by me more than all four of my own blood brothers combined. Why? Because they offered me something my own siblings could not: *They deliberately wanted and chose me.*

Charlie Dackerman and Todd Pinther lived around the corner from my house on Hanover Drive in San Jose, California. All three of us went to John Muir Elementary and in the teen years attended Miller Junior High and Lynbrook High School—all which were within four blocks of each other. We "clicked" mostly because we had the same passions: riding our bikes everywhere, playing football, exploring, creating havoc, and going to the grocery store to buy candy and gum. That was our foundation.

There was a creek behind my house, a wonderland of alligator lizards, frogs, little rivers, tree forts, and the world's largest bathroom. With just a little effort, we could rapidly expand our rapscallion network to a second circle of neighborhood boys. Especially if a football game was called, if we drafted armies for mock battles, or if we wanted to play sardines (a hide-and-seek game), word would go out, and boys everywhere ran to the spot, like playground kids to a fistfight. In fact, you could actually track how many "followers" we had by counting the number of bikes on my front lawn. Bikes, buddies, adventurers, and mischief in our little–big world of West San Jose.

The other reason we clicked was for the exact opposite reason: We were very different. Charlie's family was from New York. He had a noticeable accent, a totally different family culture, and was opinionated. The day he landed in my third-grade class as the new kid, Mrs. Roddy asked for a volunteer to show him around school for the day; for some reason I cannot explain, I raised my hand, and we wound up sticking together like Velcro straps from that day on. Todd, on the other hand, was the middle linebacker on our Pee Wee Tackle Football team. He feared no one and was feared by everyone on the playground because he was so tough. He was never mean or a bully. You just did not want to tangle with Todd. And to my recollection, nobody ever did. We connected through football and a shared love of the Minnesota Vikings. Together, we led the charge to organize games.

As for me, I had a cross-cultural family—a Pacific Islander mom and a southern dad and seven kids unpeacefully coexisting on Hanover Drive. My house was crazy, full of foreign lingo and accents, different customs, island music, a non-American menu of food, and a mom always eager to put food in your mouth or play cards. Deep down, I was always afraid that my crazy cross-cultural life would be weird to Charlie and Todd. But, just like when I was at their house, it was more like an anthropology study in how other "tribes" lived. By God's design, we discovered each other, aligned our passions, and engaged the differences with eyes wide open in a spirit of brotherhood.

Right now, Jesus Christ is creating an ever-growing community of Christ-following men you would never group together. They are hipster and corporate, inner city and suburb, West Coast and East Coast, black and white. Formerly individuals with some kind of cultural label, they are starting to "click," show up in each other's lives, seek fellowship, chase adventure, and muster large groups of like-minded friends in one spot. The fight is on, and they don't want to miss the spectacle. This phenomenon is happening because they have the same passion: a radical and transcendent love for Jesus Christ. He is the most important thing in their lives and has taken over their bodies, their identities, their money, their visions, and their futures.

This movement is happening exactly *because* it is made up of different tribes of men. The differences are making the movement richer, stronger, and even more fearless. They are not like each other on many levels, but they are "as one" on the most important thing: They are sons of the King.

Fellowships are forming because the King is coming. God is calling together sincere hearts, strong energy, and a transcendent brand of masculinity—the Spirit-empowered kind—that culture has not seen on this scale since Pentecost. It will involve Kingdom mischief, where brothers will be seeking out brothers to plan and execute risk-filled adventures for God and goodness. There's a certain quality to these men that Jesus loves too:

> Jesus said, "Let the little children come to me, and do not hinder them, for the kingdom of heaven belongs to such as these."[1]

> Truly I tell you, anyone who will not receive the kingdom of God like a little child will never enter it.[2]

They have the spirit of the rapscallion—a community of men ready to cause some Kingdom mischief at a moment's notice in the power of His Spirit.

This is your community.

Shaping and Sharpening

Victory or defeat is determined in most men's lives by the friends they choose.

That powerful fact is being played out in your life right

now, with consequences for the Kingdom of God. God calls His dangerous good to examine their first circle of friendships to determine if the driving force behind them is Jesus Christ and if the goal of that fellowship of men is to become like Him. I like the relationship X-ray Timothy Keller advises all followers of Jesus to put their friendships through: "Spiritual friendship is . . . eagerly helping one another know, serve, love, and resemble God in deeper and deeper ways."[3]

What does your X-ray reveal? For the dangerous good, resembling Christ is God's main goal in your life.

> We know that in all things God works for the good of those who love him, who have been called according to his purpose. For those God foreknew he also predestined to be conformed to the image of his Son, that he might be the firstborn among many brothers and sisters.[4]

"All things" means we do not compartmentalize God's purposes. All circumstances and relationships are sacred, working toward the goal of Christlikeness. "Many brothers" means God wants a *movement* of Christlikeness that gives Him glory in the world. Consider your community of male friendships: They are either dulling you to God's vision or sharpening you to His goals.

Seeing your friendships in this bigger picture changes everything about how you approach your friendships as opposed to your acquaintances and neighbors, whom God has called you to love and reach for Jesus. God says there are eternal consequences to the company you keep and that reaching His destination will be directly affected by the nature of your affiliations.

> You will walk in the way of good men
> And keep to the paths of the righteous.[5]

> He who walks with wise men will be wise,
> But the companion of fools will suffer harm.[6]

Walking is a biblical metaphor for friendship; experiencing life together is a journey. Let it sink into your mind: Your God is a friendship—Father, Son, and Holy Spirit—and He has made you in His image for the purpose of experiencing friendship at this same level. Simple, strong, and transformational friendship is life. That is why when we are not doing relationships right, we feel like we are not doing life right!

Intentionality in a dangerous good circle of friends involves honesty with God, honesty with yourself, and ultimately, some life-changing honesty. The stakes are that high, and your community of men is that powerful in God's Kingdom agenda for this hour in history. The rails that dangerous community runs on—taking you to Christlikeness—are clear, few, strong, and transformational. But for these same reasons, they will demand discipline and faith.

Christlikeness through community demands discipline

because, unlike other relationships that are automatically built into your life fabric (for example, marriage, family, and work), friendships require intentionality. Friendships are usually the first thing that gets squeezed out of life. To this end, dangerous good communities will most likely involve a lifestyle change that needs to be valued and guarded. You are going to have to say no to some things in order to say yes to more regular, intentional, Spirit-empowered friendships.

To do so will demand faith, because you are going to have to give up trusting self (which, ironically, makes the acronym GUTS.) and believe God will shape and sharpen you in this community. Your space will be invaded. You will be known. You will be challenged to become like Christ. Your maturity will be tested, along with your commitment to grow. All those things do require some spiritual faith and personal guts. But as you trust God by trusting the family of brothers in Christ, your character will keep pace with your influence, your leadership will be less synthetic and more authentic, and God's Word will cease being just good information and come alive as His direct revelation to you.

Dangerous good communities of men are composed of men with daring faith that pushes its ranks to stretch in order to live the gospel of Jesus Christ.

> [Jesus said,] "If you try to hang on to your life,
> you will lose it. But if you give up your life for my
> sake and for the sake of the Good News, you will
> save it."[7]

If there is never an uncomfortable moment for you in a dangerous good community of men, then you are not with God's rapscallions up to no bad. There must be a tension inside of you in order for an advance of Christlikeness to take place in you. Tension means something is going to happen.

Let Community Come

Think of dangerous good community as a refinery where Christlikeness is forged.

You know you are in the right company when there is a sense that strong, solid, long-lasting character is being pounded out. The energy of this spiritual furnace is fueled by the pure motivations to honor the sacrifice of Christ and pour out commitments into His mold. The willingness to withstand the heat of accountability and the pressure of being shaped into a useful instrument for God has a multiplying effect on all present. Heated, cooled, pounded, and sharpened over and over—this process produces men who are ready to be placed in the hands of God to bring justice and hope by their very presence. The process involves transparency, proximity, and frequency.

Transparency: The First Rail

The first rail of dangerous good community is the principle of transparency. Many men are winning the battle of images and losing the battles of life. They have amazing reputations in their fields, and among their social networks, even as their lives are falling apart. How is this possible? They are not actually *known*. They do not let others into their real life—the one that struggles with impulses within or forces without. The deep fear that people will see their real life keeps them from winning the growth God wants for us, keeps them from receiving the help of their brothers, keeps them under the power of their secret. Whatever a man can't talk about already controls him.

Dangerous good communities believe that the truest thing about dealing with sin and struggles is what God says is true. Keeping them hidden from God and your brothers is not the plan; walking in the light before God and before trusted brothers is His way. Friendship with God and your dangerous good brothers involves honesty about your real life versus the one you want to project and have people believe. Transparency is not an event or a moment of exposure to be endured but a lifestyle God has called you to. This is how God's men do life with God and with each other.

> God is light; in him there is no darkness at all. If we
> claim to have fellowship with him and yet walk in
> the darkness, we lie and do not live out the truth.
> But if we walk in the light, as he is in the light, we
> have fellowship with one another, and the blood of
> Jesus, his Son, purifies us from all sin.[8]

> Whoever conceals their sins does not prosper,
> but the one who confesses and renounces them
>   finds mercy.[9]

Confess your sins to each other and pray for each
other so that you may be healed. The prayer of
a righteous person is powerful and effective.[10]

God has dangerous good communities work this way
for a couple of strong reasons. First, your secrets reveal the
type of man you do *not* want to be. Think about it for a
second. We discuss our aspirations but we hide our trans-
gressions. Why? Because the perception plays better than
the reality. The man we hide is the man we don't want
to be. That's why God calls all His sons to risk revealing,
start transforming, and begin defeating the things that are
defeating them—by the power of the Holy Spirit, through
the counsel of His Word, and with the supporting power
of the body of Christ.

Second, your secrets give the devil power. Reflect on
this too. The unconfessed and unknown life is an isolated
life. And in the context of warfare, alone means vulnerable.
Vulnerable to the lie that if you are honest with your community of men they will reject you. Vulnerable to the lie that
no one else struggles with the issues you do. Vulnerable to
self-deceiving thoughts that rationalize and justify sin. And
on and on. Transparency breaks the power of the devil in a
man's life—which is what dangerous good community is all
about: defeating the Liar by being in the truth.

Confession (the moment of transparency we're describing
here) brings God's power into the believer's life because it
requires humility and faith—two things God loves to reward.

Satan will never tell you that confession and transparency result in power; he wants to keep you in bondage! Listen to a man who heard God's call to transparency and worked it out in a dangerous good way:

> [The Lord] said to me, "My grace is sufficient for you, for my power is made perfect in weakness." Therefore I will boast all the more gladly about my weaknesses, so that Christ's power may rest on me.[11]

The apostle Paul had an imperfect past and had learned that while confession wasn't manly in his culture, it was godly and powerful. *Transparency* is the lifestyle of the dangerous good and a hallmark of their community.

Proximity: The Second Rail

The second rail of dangerous good community is the principle of proximity—nearness. There is simply no substitute. Just ask a quarterback and his center, a recording star and his sound engineer, or an Everest climber and his Sherpa guide. They are in close quarters and intimately communicating. Up close and personal is the only way. They can't produce the desired outcome without proximity to each other.

God is big on His men being close enough to sense, discern, examine, confront, support, and shape each other into Christlikeness. People have to be close enough to you on a consistent enough basis to get a real sense of you and to really see you.

Dangerous good communities know that proximity is essential to progression as a man and a leader. There is no fear about my business being your business and your business being my business; we both have the same goal of becoming like Christ in every way. Proximity means both physical nearness—people who are available to you anytime—as well as a close trust and emotional security. When your back is to the wall and the chips are down, a dangerous good brother is there, asking not what happened, but "What do you need?" He's close when it counts, close when confronting needs to happen, and close when a confidence needs to be shared.

> My eyes will be on the faithful in the land,
>   that they may dwell with me;
> the one whose walk is blameless
>   will minister to me.[12]

> Iron sharpens iron,
> So one man sharpens another.[13]

> One who has unreliable friends soon comes to ruin,
> but there is a friend who sticks closer than a brother.[14]

The dangerous good will not let a brother be self-defeating. They will fight for his life in Christ. There is nothing like having strong friends close by, a call away, and knowing they will climb any mountain to get to you. They will be there to celebrate with you in victory, defend you when you are vulnerable, and bandage your wounds when you are injured. You are in it with them and they are in it with you.

Proximity is the lifestyle of the dangerous good and a hallmark of their community.

Frequency: The Third Rail

The third rail of dangerous good community is the principle of frequency. Any group that fails to meet regularly and put consistent energy toward the mission's goals will be defeated. Members will be undertrained, underdeveloped, and unprepared for the forces against them. You know it. Your brothers in Christ know it. But more importantly, God knows it and wants you to fight to secure consistent connection. You have to be able to measure and report your gains or losses individually within the fellowship, but you can't do that if you do not meet or see each other on a regular basis.

Dangerous good communities know that consistency of connection produces the shaping and sharpening results men need. It's a community that communicates to members up front that to be a part means to be consistent, that inconsistency will dilute the impact for you and the group. It's a community that advises members to pray about joining so that God Himself will impress on you the importance of consistency and you won't need to be reminded to come.

But in our frenetic and fragmented culture, where blowing things off is accepted and tolerated, this community of men must transcend the culture to consistently commit to a community that makes them like Christ.

Let us hold unswervingly to the hope we profess, for he who promised is faithful. And let us consider how we may spur one another on toward love and good deeds, not giving up meeting together, as some are in the habit of doing, but encouraging one another—and all the more as you see the Day approaching.[15]

The eye cannot say to the hand, "I don't need you!" And the head cannot say to the feet, "I don't need you!"[16]

Broken-male culture acts like men really don't need each other; to be "your own man" means you don't need input, mentoring, or sharpening. That myth doesn't apply to any other common pursuit, and so the dangerous good see right through it. The dangerous good value "together." Together for spiritual growth. Together for fun. Together to serve and be on a mission. They don't let their connections get squeezed out. They communicate to their families or girlfriends that they are better supporters when they are consistently together with their brothers. And their loved ones believe them— every week they carve out time to make it happen. They sacrifice other things because they assign a higher value to community and Christlikeness.

Frequency—that consistency of connection we've been discussing—is the lifestyle of the dangerous good and a hallmark of their community.

A Thick Fellowship

The natural outflow of community that is transparent, near, and frequent is a rare and powerful unity and authority in each other's lives. If life in Christ is an engine, dangerous good community is the oil that makes it work properly. If you are low on it, you get low performance. If you are supplied and resupplied with it, you get high performance and steady progress toward Christlikeness. A common passion for Christ is the foundation, combined with a kaleidoscope of faith and personalities to create a community that God says you need in order to be challenged, shaped, and encouraged in ways you never dreamed. Dissimilar men are mysteriously being connected by God for the larger, mutually beneficial purpose of Christlikeness. God's presence is thick when brothers connect and consecrate each other:

> Behold, how good and how pleasant it is
> For brothers to dwell together in unity!
> It is like the precious oil upon the head,
> Coming down upon the beard,
> Even Aaron's beard,
> Coming down upon the edge of his robes.
> It is like the dew of Hermon
> Coming down upon the mountains of Zion;
> For there the LORD commanded the blessing—
> life forever.[17]

Did you catch it? Oil and dew coming down, coming down, coming down! It's called a point of emphasis when the Scriptures repeat things three times in a minimal amount of text. Oil and dew were symbols of the powerful presence of God, and King David (the author of this psalm) does not want his men to miss one of the secrets to receiving and experiencing God's blessing: connecting with other men of God. In fact, the very first dangerous good men's group in the early church experienced this principle of God commanding blessing over connecting and seeking men. It happened among the Antioch rapscallions up to no bad.

> There were at Antioch, in the church that
> was there, prophets and teachers: Barnabas, and
> Simeon who was called Niger, and Lucius of Cyrene,
> and Manaen who had been brought up with Herod
> the tetrarch, and Saul. While they were ministering
> to the Lord and fasting, the Holy Spirit said, "Set
> apart for Me Barnabas and Saul for the work to
> which I have called them."[18]

Rapscallions praying and pleasing God together got orders for the revolution and release of the Kingdom. The dangerous good did their part and God did His.

The Spirit of the Lord says, *Get together and get your orders.*

Dangerous Good Conversation

Think back on some key childhood relationships. Why did you connect with those guys? What's different about your male friendships today? Why are they different?

Dangerous good connections will inevitably involve dynamic tension. How do you react to conflict in your friendships? How can you increase your tolerance for dynamic tension in your dangerous good friendships?

Which of these do you struggle with the most: transparency, proximity, or frequency? Why? What steps can you take to see victory in those struggles?

04

POWERFULLY
IMPACTED WOMEN

Dignity—the Arsonist and the Firefighters

—

*By believing in our nobler nature, women have the amazing power to
inspire us to live up to it.*

NEIL STRAUSS

I FELT LIKE AN ARSONIST AT A FIREFIGHTERS' CONVENTION.
The event was called ARISE. More than a thousand women
were seated in front of me. I did not know any of their stories. I
did not know one of their names. I did not have any insight into
their relationships with men. When you are a "men's expert" in
front of a crowd of women, tribal knowledge of broken-male
culture loads the conversation with unsettling but indisputable
realities. I could only assume that there were plenty of painful
stories connected to a man or numbers of men whose character
or conduct had impacted them negatively.

The themes I was going to focus on were nuclear: gender wars, the failure of "traditional" masculinity, the lies of

"reactive" femininity, and the emerging "third wave" of dangerous good men blazing a new trail of respect, honor, partnership, family, and world-changing impact. I had a low-grade anxiety fever. Never fails. The only advantage I have in such situations is that I know what's coming—*and they don't.*

Fast forward forty-five minutes. Against all odds, these women were on their feet clapping, and my heart rate slowly returned back to normal. The firefighters did not attack the arsonist.

Nevertheless, my hunch was right: There was a lot of hurt in the room connected to broken male character and conduct—beginning with myself.

I told them my story of having an alcoholic father whose absence made me feel like one big accident as a young boy. I invited them into my own broken quest for sonship, and all the unhealthy (but culturally endorsed) ways I was trained to validate myself as a man. I talked about how I learned to disconnect my heart from my head and injured others in the process, all the while believing I was advancing in the pecking order.

Not surprisingly, my story resonated with them—specifically, how the lies that sexual conquest, physical toughness, and net worth as the observable "end zones" of masculine glory did not provide the things I most needed to make my relationships work. Missing models and mentors in my family (the first community of acceptance) forced me to look outside for a way to be, believe, and behave that would secure worth and belonging. Unfortunately, the culturally approved ways of masculinity doomed me to creating a lot of suffering for people who would eventually connect with me. Self-gratifying, self-serving, and self-preserving behavior makes a horrible boyfriend, husband, dad, and partner for women of all ages.

They agreed. But what were women to do about men like me?

Well, they said, "Enough!"

I shared how reactive feminism was to be expected. The value of women as more than pawns and trophies of the broken male vision was absolutely needed. The goal: Dignity in! Silly double standards for women out! Most every human being agrees.

However, reactions to suffering and injustice are never solutions. In fact, riding a wave of both real and imagined injustices, the message to women over time had become *Be a better man than men themselves can be.* I explained that for 90 percent of women, this message stops being helpful and starts being hurtful the second the wedding ring goes on and babies start arriving.

Not surprisingly, a cluster of younger women (some of whom were moms) approached me after my presentation. They talked about being reared in the cultural waves of reactive femininity and how the quest for independence from men had ended up creating massive emotional and relational conflicts in their lives. The feminine power message failed to help them, and confusion set in.

Both men and women are hurting, lonely, and set adrift by a culture without any meaningful social forces creating space and conversation to transcend the situation and bring us together. Can you imagine CNN or Fox News reporting on a headline that read: "NEW MOVEMENT SWEEPS INTO LOCAL COMMUNITIES: WOMEN CHAMPIONING MEN"? That would be a different national discussion, wouldn't it? Hard to conceive seeing or hearing something like that against the cultural backdrop of women marching and protesting against the darker caricatures of men that dominate the news cycle. In this moment of history, traditional "broken" masculinity is out. But reactive femininity is also getting a lot of pushback, and from a source you would never expect: women.

Into these gender doldrums a fresh wind is starting to fill the sails of a new vision. The dangerous good wave of masculinity, and a corresponding wave of femininity, can be seen rising above the gender war. It's not a reaction; it's a solution! It doesn't seek to garner power and control or create distance; it seeks to accomplish the important goals of living as men and women in partnership with each other.

This new vision explains things. It is a breath of fresh air. It eliminates competition and creates connection. It heals wounds and brings unity. It's a different dimension that traditionalism and feminism cannot touch exactly because it originates in the *Kingdom of God*.

In that realm, dangerous good men rise from the ashes of humiliation to honor women, lift them up, and lead them like Jesus.

The result? A victory for the sexes and the defeat of an enemy.

Follow You, Follow Me

Diamonds are precious because they are rare and hard to mine.

In the Bible's book of Judges, you encounter a diamond of a story that is rare for any age of human history. It is a very public example of a man who rises above culture to dignify and partner with a strong woman. In a welcomed twist, the woman agrees, loves it, and celebrates the partnership. This victory of a man and woman actually working with each other versus against each other gives the dangerous good community a clear reflection of what God wants to do right now in the body of Christ to defeat evil and advance His purposes.

The main character of this unparalleled moment in biblical history is a woman of God named Deborah. She is unique among the women of faith in the Bible in that she was the first (and only) female ever called on by God to lead the people of Israel. Serving as both a prophet and judge, Deborah was called in a difficult time; the Israelites were being cruelly oppressed by King Jabin of Canaan and desperately pleading with God for deliverance. The Lord answered, telling Deborah to call on and send a dangerously good man named Barak to battle against the powerful Canaanite commander Sisera. What follows is a tense and prophetic parable for the dangerous good revolution.

It goes normally at first. Deborah summons Barak and issues her request. Barak agrees but gives her a condition that she must meet before one sword is drawn. He looks right at her and says, "If you go with me, I will go; but if you don't go with me, I won't go."[1]

What a moment! If you think bringing a woman into the field of battle is a big issue today, imagine a time when it was incomprehensible. But Barak rose above a mountain of cultural, historical, political, and professional obstacles to proactively invite a strong woman into partnership for God's higher purposes and for the sake of others. It was countercultural and not "manly" in his time exactly because it was godly. Deborah hesitates, takes a deep breath, agrees, and together they proceed to execute a plan that would free the Israelites, advance God's plan, and defeat the enemy. Deborah gets the honor of the victory over Sisera, they sing and celebrate it together, and peace is secured for the next forty years.

On the day of victory over Sisera, the "Song of Deborah and Barak" is sung together by these unlikely partners who broke all the rules of their culture for a higher purpose. Note that. Now listen to the heart of a woman who appreciates both the strength and leadership of a man and the young men who fought with him.

On that day Deborah and Barak son of Abinoam
sang this song:

"When the princes in Israel take the lead,
when the people willingly offer themselves—
praise the LORD!

Hear this, you kings! Listen, you rulers!
I, even I, will sing to the LORD;
I will praise the LORD, the God of Israel, in song."²

She was the leader but she recognized that the "princes"
(the young men of Israel under Barak) needed to suit up,
show up, and take the lead! Seeing and experiencing that was,
for her, cause for an end zone dance, high fives, and hugs
for strangers! She was shouting from the rooftops that her
men needed to be both feared and celebrated. Thank God
Almighty—men taking the lead at last!

Deborah represents hundreds of millions of women
worldwide who also are waiting for the "princes" to take the
lead and fight for them, their well-being, their families, and
their community in the Spirit of Christ.

Barak's strong actions with his young men and Deborah's
willingness to trust and come alongside them present a
spiritually powerful scenario for the dangerous good community and the women affected by them to consider.
What would happen if God's men and God's women rose
above gender wars, passive-aggressive activism, and mutually exclusive spiritual communities and fought together
as one against the real enemy? Barak answered Deborah's
call to work together for *God's purpose*, he obeyed *God's
plan*, and in doing so, he demonstrated a version of masculinity that this generation of men can learn from in a few
specific ways.

Lesson One: Be Humble

Today, men need to recognize they are not islands. We need help—female help. Barak wouldn't go to war without Deborah's involvement and spiritual wisdom. Although he led the battle, he viewed her presence and mind as vital to securing victory. What a great message to her: "I am not going unless you go with me." I wish I could have seen the look on her face and the exchange of spirits between them. Shoulder to shoulder they approached the battle lines, and back to back they went into the fight—the prophet praying, watching, and advising alongside the warrior amid the sound of clashing metal. Barak's humility secured the victory; his pride would have destroyed it. The clear message to Deborah: *I need you!*

That's God's plan for the dangerous good man with respect to women.

> If you've gotten anything at all out of following Christ, if his love has made any difference in your life, if being in a community of the Spirit means anything to you, if you have a heart, if you *care*— then do me a favor: Agree with each other, love each other, be deep-spirited friends. Don't push your way to the front; don't sweet-talk your way to the top. Put yourself aside, and help others get ahead. Don't be obsessed with getting your own advantage. Forget yourselves long enough to lend a helping hand.[3]

Only one attitude can get us there: humility.

In families, dating relationships, marriage, the workplace, and, most importantly, as believers in Jesus Christ, this kind of attitude and thinking rises above culture and into Christlikeness in the most relevant way today. How different would relationships between men and women be if both genders thought that way and sent that message to one another? How would it impact the discussion about men if women felt seen, valued, and partnered with versus dismissed, minimized, or thought less of? Who are the men and women commissioned to come together, think together, and stand together to win victories for Christ and humanity?

Believing men and women must run to battle—*together*.

Lesson Two: Don't Grumble the Opportunity Away

Barak accepted Deborah's call to face a powerful and daunting opponent. It was a moment of decision for him; he could have rationalized, grumbled about the numbers (the enemy had more chariots), and excused himself from consideration. But he didn't. Instead, in faith, he looked for the God opportunity within this challenge. He acted like a man and did the smartest thing he could have possibly done—he invited a smart, spiritually strong, and wise partner into the battle plan.

How would women respond to a modern man like that? How baffled would culture-at-large be to see men and women fighting side by side and back to back against common evils versus against each other? How would God be glorified by a movement of men who see the opportunity within today's gender malaise to see and partner with their girlfriends, wives, daughters, sisters in Christ, and women in general to win a larger victory for God? The dangerous good are being called to choose partnership, match strengths, and go into battle with our women for the glory of God.

That, too, is God's plan for the dangerous good with respect to women.

> Do everything readily and cheerfully—no bickering, no second-guessing allowed! Go out into the world uncorrupted, a breath of fresh air in this squalid and polluted society. Provide people with a glimpse of good living and of the living God. Carry the light-giving Message into the night so I'll have good cause to be proud of you on the day that Christ returns.[4]

The gender wars are raging and sometimes it feels like we are outgunned, outnumbered, and underappreciated. But the dangerous good community of men recognize the opportunity within the challenge. The current gender climate can be positively confronted and leveraged for God's glory through a new willingness to see and partner with our sisters. This movement will be a glimpse of God and a breath of fresh air for all the world to take in.

Lesson Three: Know Thyself

Barak knew his strengths and weaknesses. His strength was leading men, but he did not have the wisdom or connection to God that Deborah did. He was a general; she was a judge and prophet. He saw her strength and decided to put it to work right alongside his—brilliant. Brilliant because his pride wasn't in the driver's seat. Brilliant because he knew his limitations. Brilliant because he didn't let his fears of disapproval by his fellow generals and soldiers sabotage this out-of-the-box partnership. Brilliant because it brought a new asset into play that would help bring victory.

Smart men honor, dignify, and partner with great women to achieve far more than they ever would by themselves. God said it in the beginning and it is just as true now as it was the first time He declared it.

> "It's not good for the Man to be alone; I'll make him
> a helper, a companion." . . .
> GOD put the Man into a deep sleep. As he slept
> he removed one of his ribs and replaced it with
> flesh. GOD then used the rib that he had taken from
> the Man to make Woman and presented her to
> the Man.[5]

God could have formed woman out of Adam's toe, so he could look down on her. He could have formed her out of Adam's hair, so she would have to look up at him. But instead, He chose to form her out of his rib, *so she could be alongside him.* Woman was placed next to man—not below him, not above him, but alongside him to reflect the same unity God Himself enjoys in the Trinity.

Israel was led by a woman—one who needed masculine strength. Barak led a fighting legion—one that needed feminine strength. So he accepted the call of his hour, and together they won the battle. Today, Spirit-filled masculinity that follows in Barak's footsteps is what will foment revolution where it counts the most: in homes, neighborhoods, and workplaces in real time. It is in these spaces where the meaning of the dangerous good movement really lies, valuing what women can bring to the table in every dimension of life and work.

The next time you feel like you are facing a challenge alone, be secure enough in your own masculinity to partner creatively with a strong woman God has placed in your life. Together, you can win a bigger victory than you ever could achieve by yourself.

As dangerous good men see and invite female strength into the fabric of life in Christ and as men, women will be blessed, honored, helped, and activated to be a new voice for men. Jesus did all those things for women He lived among. He walked into a broken-male culture that thanked God daily that they were not born as women and replaced that mind-set with behaviors and actions that dignified women. Secure in the Father, He knew He would turn the gender disparity on its head in a Spirit-filled, unifying way that affirms strengths. The women watching Christ and the men of Pentecost not only loved this new brand of Spirit-filled masculinity but also evangelized it among all their friends and families, becoming key accelerators for the early church.

God says women complete men: They supply exactly what we lack in perspective, intuition, and Holy Spirit gifting. They are powerful creations and even more powerful when partnering alongside a Christlike man. More eternally, women are a critical piece in God's perfect plans, to be recognized in the world through the body of Christ. You don't have to be married and you don't have to sexualize His intention. You simply have to see women the way God sees them. Only arrogance or stupidity would sabotage a man's willingness to benefit from that blessing.

The oxygen that fuels the fire of the dangerous good revolution will increasingly be the voices of women who have experienced the blessing of partnership with Christlike men. Because they are experiencing the caring, strong, and positive impact of Christlike men, these beautiful partners will aggressively champion the dangerous good fellowship. They are evangelists and connectors for what they have experienced. I have seen the excitement in their faces when I talk about this movement. When I talk at women's conferences about the dangerous good rising and poll them about a new wave of spiritually and relationally healthy men, they rise up, literally, and applaud. Their energy is palpable. This is especially true among Millennial women who are eagerly seeking and wanting to support the movement. They perceive it as great for the gospel and equally beneficial for them. If Millennial men increasingly choose to identify with Christ, pursue that identity and community, and connect those pursuits for the benefit of women and children, thermonuclear appreciation ensues. The thought among women is: *Finally!*

That was the sentiment when women encountered Jesus. And just as all women of all ages do when they encounter something they like, they wasted no time telling their girlfriends about this man who was so different in His treatment of women. Like a wildfire, story after story spread: the woman at the well, the confronting of men who twisted the law for easy divorces, saving an adulterous woman from being stoned, the healing of the hemorrhaging woman, the woman whom Jesus said would be immortalized for blessing Him long after the Pharisees were dead, and many others. The word was out among women young and old. Huddles and whispers exploded the reports up and down Palestine about one man breaking all the rules of broken-male culture.

What might the women have said about Him? What had they heard? What did they think about this man who, according to reports, protected, dignified, elevated, and honored women in such a radical way? One thing is for certain, based on the Gospel narratives: They finally felt like they had a champion.

More significantly, a new mold for masculinity was being birthed—one that addressed the root problem preventing partnership and robbing dignity. Jesus had followers who were men. Would they be like Him?

The answer was yes. Women now had an army of champions in the mold of Jesus. The male culture that caused women so much pain and suffering was confronted by a new kind of man, a different breed, a dangerously good community of Spirit-empowered men who took care of, welcomed, and partnered alongside women in the fastest advance of the gospel earth has ever seen. They were as one.

Hundreds of millions of women are ready for today's dangerous good movement to catch fire the way that first one did. They've been fighting the fires of broken-male culture, but they will welcome an army of arsonists who are up to no bad. They are waiting to vocalize their appreciation and support of men who are dangerous with goodness like Christ.

For their part, the dangerous good have the greatest chance to shine the light of Christ for the sake of women exactly because the backdrop is so dark. The voices of women will be the secret sauce of the next masculine revolution.

The only cautionary warning is this: It starts with your identity, your community, and their dignity all colliding for the glory of God in the Spirit of Christ. It will be history in the making; you'll see for yourself as you commit to Christlikeness.

Watch.

Dangerous Good Conversation

—

Have you ever felt like an arsonist at a firefighters' convention? How has the feminist reaction against broken masculinity affected you personally—in your relationship with a spouse or girlfriend? With female coworkers? At church?

What appeals to you about the partnership of Barak and Deborah? What impact could you envision if you had a similar partnership with a woman in your life?

Which of the three lessons do you struggle most with: humility, grumbling, or self-awareness? Why? What will help you grow in this area?

05

POWERFULLY AFFECTED CHILDREN

Legacy—Worth and Peace

—

It's easier to build strong children than to repair broken men.

FREDERICK DOUGLASS

I DID *NOT* WANT TO BRING THIS REPORT CARD HOME.

The grades were not so hot, but it was the "Teacher's Comment" section that caught my attention: *Kenny is a bright student at times, but he has diarrhea of the mouth.*

Seriously? It's really funny to retell this story for a laugh now, but when you are eight years old it was confusing and scary to have an adult rip on you. My eight-year-old eyes read it again and confirmed the irrevocable and unchangeable assessment of a respected adult about me. It was my first experience of being self-conscious. Even as a third grader, I could easily discern the feelings behind the sentiment my teacher was wanting to project onto my parents about their son. Namely, *Your son has potential, but mostly he is a disruptive and disrespectful blabbermouth with no self-awareness.* I didn't possess the words to articulate that feeling, but I knew this was not a positive report; I was the source of negative feelings inside of others.

I feel for my third-grade teacher (and for all teachers, for that matter) because she was not a marriage, family, and child counselor who could wave a wand and fix the insides of a home, a family dynamic, a dad's absenteeism, and alcoholism. She could not satisfy a little boy's broken quest for someone—anyone—to see and talk to him. If you are a mentor, a teacher, a coach, or a dad, there is a huge lesson here with respect to human behavior: *Problems seldom reside at the level at which you finally see them.* A problem behavior didn't start at the moment you observed it; it started sometime in the past and built up to that moment. Men and magma. Again.

So it was with me.

As a career mental-health professional and now as a pastor, I have a ton of compassion for children thrust into the social matrix without any positive mentors and with a terrifyingly low sense of self. I don't want to dwell on the metaphor too much, but there is one last profound lesson to be gained from my teacher's reference to diarrhea: Diarrhea is not a disease; it's a symptom. Something foreign finds its way inside you, starts messing with your insides, and then manifests itself outside in a recognizable and unhealthy way. Same for me back then and same for all children walking planet earth with a lingering sense that they are not seen nor valued. They will project those feelings and the related fears into behaviors that make them visible to others. Too often, they will be labeled, their loneliness turned into a diagnosis or exploited. My label was ADHD, but the root cause, the real problem, was family chaos and dysfunction, brought on largely by the choices of my father.

My personal diary of the "diarrhea report card" story is funny and serious, and it provides insight into how the dangerous good can impact the world in a powerful way. It is funny in the sense that that's what I was like to have in class from my teacher's perspective: unplanned and uncontrolled talking that messed up lesson plans, class order, and her supply of sanity. Thus, her diarrhea imagery: No one wants or plans for it, and when you have it, it's like having a roadside bomb in your body that may go off unpredictably!

On the flip side, my story is very serious: Families form people, and men play a huge role in determining the emotional health of children, influencing their life trajectories, relationships, and spiritual journey. Using another image that men can appreciate: Children stand, for better or for worse, in the direct blast zone of adult male choices and character. That powerful fact has massive implications for the dangerous good revolution. Children are most deeply affected, positively and negatively, by the heart, character, and conduct of the men placed in their lives.

Perhaps you have never thought about the connection between children and the choices of men before, but justice for most children on planet earth is one good man away. Similarly, *injustice* is one selfish man away. Consider this:

- 80 percent of males 18–49 who have no children say they want to have children.[1]
- 47 percent of all men will father a child.[2]
- 70,000,000 men in the United States are fathers.[3]
- 27 percent of American children live separated from their father.[4]
- 171,000,000 children in the world are orphans, currently living without parents.[5]
- 40,000,000–42,000,000 people throughout the world are prostitutes, 75 percent of whom are between the ages of 13 and 25.[6]

When you look at these figures, two things should happen: *Your blood should boil and your heart should break.* The blast zone of the dangerous good revolution worldwide quite literally impacts the future of hundreds of millions of children by virtue of the proximity children have to the choices men make.

That enormity has never been lost on God, who tracks the behavior of His sons and their blast zones of impact on women and children.

For the vineyard of the LORD of hosts is the house
    of Israel
And the men of Judah His delightful plant.

Thus He looked for justice, but behold, bloodshed;
For righteousness, but behold, a cry of distress.[7]

"He looked" reflects an intentional inspection. There is everyone in the faith community (*the vineyard*) and then there are God's sons (*the men of Judah*). His sons are the object of fatherly pride in this image (*His delightful plant*) that He wants to show off to everyone who would visit His house. Like any father, He is looking for a reflection of the best parts of Himself in His boys (*He looked for justice . . . For righteousness*), but He finds the exact opposite. The fruit of this plant is plainly and disappointingly *un*delightful (*behold, bloodshed . . . behold, a cry of distress*).

That should send shivers down your spine. As men of God assigned to a generation of women and children, we are purposed to bless. God is watching His sons, tracking their actions with respect to others they are connected to, and expecting them to deliver His justice and righteousness to them.

Man to man, God wants to see a family resemblance in us that communicates to a watching world that His dangerous good boys are up to no bad, bringing what is due to those He has entrusted them to influence. If compassion is due, His sons bring it. If protection is due, His sons deliver. If dignity is due, the same. The God who loves justice and righteousness has a team on earth tasked with manifesting it—or so He hopes.

We are going to address how the dangerous good revolution will finally show the world what true justice for all looks and feels like through Spirit-filled men's community later. But since the majority of men both want a child and will have blood or other relationships with children (uncles, coaches, teachers, mentors, youth leaders, etc.), we first need to consider specifically how our blast zone of impact will reflect the Father and be a witness to His Kingdom rule in our lives. Justice for hundreds of millions of children is on the horizon.

This time, God's "delightful plant" will be in a full, glorious bloom.

The Power of Seeing and Believing

To be seen.

Hardwired into the heart of all children is a longing to be noticed, appreciated, known. The problem is that someone has to stop, take notice, and commit energy to expressing acknowledgment personally, in a meaningful way. The tragic irony is that today, being seen has never been easier and, at the same time, never been so meaningless. Digital symbols, conversations, sentiments, and connections have created an epic hunger for real intimacy in people of all ages. Try as we may, the planet is having great difficulty fording the fast-flowing river of social information to reach the other side—the human side. But for those who can somehow "make a moment" with others, the difference personally, relationally, and emotionally pierces the soul: *I see you.* These sacred spaces of time are the true diamonds of interaction among the costume fakeries we let pass for social connection today.

But how can the dangerous good deliver these diamonds, create these spaces, and transcend culture without having seen or experienced them in our own lives? How do I do it with my own children?

Witness the Father.

> As soon as Jesus was baptized, he went up out of
> the water. At that moment heaven was opened,
> and he saw the Spirit of God descending like a dove
> and alighting on him. And a voice from heaven said,
> "This is my Son, whom I love; with him I am well
> pleased."[8]

These words didn't need to be spoken. The Father, Son, and Holy Spirit are intimately connected already; they are not needy or broken and in need of repair. This event was for our sake—to *show us* how we can achieve, experience, and reproduce that same intimacy of the Trinity in our own hearts and in our own relationships with all those we are called to love. And while God's modeling here shows us what every human (especially a child) needs from the men in their lives, if you want to be a father or already have kids, *pay very close attention* by asking yourself two powerful questions:

1. Have I personally experienced what is being described?
2. Am I following God's example with the children He has placed under my care?

An explosive witness for Christ is coming when this generation of God's men meet these dangerous needs in children's lives the way God meets them for His own Son.

A Dangerous Need: Experiencing a Strong Moment

"At that moment heaven was opened, and he saw the Spirit of God descending like a dove and alighting on him." Timing is everything. Jesus is flushing water out of His eyes, John the Baptist is trying to lift a grown man above the waterline, crowds of people are gathered around. To everyone's surprise, time is stopped, and a personal moment between a father and son is publicly broadcast for all to witness. It is clearly planned. It is clearly initiated. It is clearly intentional. It is clearly impactful. It is clearly personal. There is no escaping this moment. What follows is a previously secret flood of thought, feelings, and emotions bursting into real time in order to answer one question for all time: *Does anyone closely connected to Jesus actually see and appreciate Jesus?*

What we witness is a strong father creating a strong moment for an exchange of hearts—one giving and the other receiving. He does it again in Matthew 17. Moments like this are rare in today's social matrix. Don't get me wrong: To be sure there is a lot of celebrating—plenty of fanfare among "friends." These external connections are easy, but if the heart connection is missing, the power is missing. While an interaction may have happened person to person, the connection is hollow, empty, and without lasting significance.

By contrast, you know a strong moment with God or a fellow human has occurred when you feel affirmed for who you are without comparison or reference to anyone or anything else. The result: intimacy and peace. The doubt is gone.

If people—especially children—don't receive authentically strong moments like that, they will, out of fear, move to create their own moments of recognition in unhealthy ways. The soul needs filling, which is why we call such an adult or child needy. In the absence of strong moments, a sense of specialness, and the peace emanating from this connection from a father or father figure, the need to know takes over.

The National Center for Fatherhood research suggests that a broken quest to be seen and accepted in some form of community ensues until it is found, regardless of the potential negative or harmful natures of those communities. Fatherless children are

- twice as likely to be incarcerated;
- four times more likely to have an out-of-wedlock birth;
- twice as likely to drop out of high school;
- four times more likely to commit suicide;
- 90 percent of the homeless and runaway population;
- 80 percent of violent rapists; and
- 63 percent of youth suicides.[9]

Because God knows exactly how He made us, that fathers would abandon their own, and that gaping holes of the soul would be produced, He orchestrated a massive moment in time to let all men know for all time that He sees us and loves us personally.

> For God so loved the world that he gave his one and
> only Son, that whoever believes in him shall not
> perish but have eternal life.[10]

It is the most famous verse in the Bible for a very good reason: It is "the moment" we all long for. At the heart of the gospel is the heart of a Father who couldn't stand the idea that any of His creations would not *be seen* and *feel their worth*. So He initiated and intentionally sent us a message in a moment that we could see, feel, internalize, and accept so that we could experience worth and peace. This experience with the Father, this adoption into the family of God, this encounter is the bedrock of the dangerous good revolution both personally and interpersonally. From the Father's perspective, it's silly for you to make futile or vain attempts to be seen and get the approval of man when you are already seen, believed in, and intentionally loved by the One who matters most. You are secure.

Similarly, children need to be seen, believed in, intentionally loved, and secured on the inside by the man in their lives that matters most—their father (blood or otherwise).

By His own example, God says we need a strong moment of acceptance from Him and we need to create strong personal moments of acceptance for children.

A Dangerous Need: Receiving a Strong Name

"And a voice from heaven said, 'This is my Son.'" After the best moment of public recognition in human history (the heavens opening, the Holy Spirit gently falling upon Jesus like a dove, and a supernatural light targeting on Jesus), the best words ever spoken to a man started to follow. The pride is palpable and the exchange of hearts begins.

"This is my Son." What every human being craves—especially children—is to be personally and enthusiastically claimed by name. In this moment, God has everyone's attention: Now what? He says what every child hopes the one person they look up to the most will say: *He's mine.*

Why such possessiveness? Stating the family connection between the Father and His Son is important on two important levels. First, the words *This is my Son* assign a unique position. Since God claims Jesus as His Son, Jesus can claim all that is God's. All of God's authority, all of God's resources, all of God's power, and all of God's privileges are fully available to Jesus. Imagine the pride of being able to say, "My Dad is the CEO of everything."

Second, the words *This is my Son* assign a unique identity. All that is true about God's character can be found in the Son. Jesus will have the family resemblance and a fierce loyalty to the family expression. When people are publicly declared family members, it creates both a responsibility and an expectation to represent that family. His Spirit gets reflected to the world.

For those who are led by the Spirit of God are the children of God. The Spirit you received does not make you slaves, so that you live in fear again; rather, the Spirit you received brought about your adoption to sonship. And by him we cry, "*Abba*, Father." The Spirit himself testifies with our spirit that we are God's children. Now if we are children, then we are heirs—heirs of God and co-heirs with Christ, if indeed we share in his sufferings in order that we may also share in his glory.[11]

As Christ followers, we receive the name God has given us as well: "My Son." We have become His through Christ, positionally. By His own example, God declares sonship over Jesus and over us. You are God's son, with full access as well as full responsibilities.

Having had this experience ourselves with God, the dangerous good community of men recognizes that all children need to be personally claimed, positioned by their relationship to us to succeed, and empowered to reflect the best parts of us.

A Dangerous Need: Receiving a Strong Love

God proceeds to issue His second power declaration over and about Jesus in front of the crowd. "This is my son, whom I love." Whereas the pride of the Father–Son connection could be felt in the first statement ("This is my son"), the heart of the father would be felt in the second ("whom I love"). In context, it reflects for all time what every man, woman, and child needs to hear and experience: unconditional love, or *acceptance without performance.*

These words are spoken over Jesus at His baptism. Jesus has yet to preach one sermon, heal one leper, cast out one demon, do one miracle, call one follower, forgive one sinner, or endure one moment of suffering. Being the object of such unconditional love and acceptance from the Father made Jesus fearless before men and able to offer the same type of love to all kinds of people, people who felt marginalized because they were labeled "sinners" and "not good enough" for God to love them. The power of unconditional acceptance, as we see in Jesus after this moment, is total freedom to serve, connect, touch, engage, care, witness, and die for our sake *secure in the Father's love.*

The same unconditional love is ours as well. God does not love us based on our performance. When love in a relationship is based on performance, the foundation of the relationship erodes into a fatal cycle of fear. Jesus knew nothing of that fear and neither do the dangerous good. God's unconditional love for us based on Christ's work on the cross eliminates fear and replaces it with gratitude and energy rising out of thankfulness to honor His sacrificial love.

He died for all, that those who live should no
longer live for themselves but for him who died
for them and was raised again.[12]

That is the power of unconditional and sacrificial love being recognized, received, and responded to by someone. It creates a spirit of thankfulness and stewardship to honor the sacrifice. By contrast, fear of somehow losing God's love by what you do or don't do inevitably devolves into performance for God's favor and love. That is when our spiritual life hits a slippery slope God never intended. Performance for God's favor and love leads to competition and judgment because there is a limited supply reserved only for the best. Competition and judgment creates standards that have to be met. Those who are meeting them are accepted and those who don't are treated as second class, which causes division between people and distance from God.

Jesus called the Pharisees hypocrites because they could never live up to their own standards—let alone the Lord's—while, at the same time, demanding other people live up to those standards. Oddly, His unconditional love violated their sense of fairness; they found it difficult to break out of their prideful performance mode, which Jesus labeled "heavy, cumbersome loads."[13]

The best gift a dangerous good man can give to a child is a love not based on what they do or don't do. By His own example, God has modeled that, and Jesus modeled internalizing and walking powerfully in that love. Give to children what God has given you—the inner security of acceptance without performance. This helps them solve the one inner struggle the evil one loves to perpetuate in the little spirits of children: the acceptance issue. They need to know they will never lose your love, no matter what they do.

Children have simple and powerful filters for internalizing and recognizing whether or not they are worthy of love.

1. TIME: Isn't that how we assess if anyone truly cares about anyone else? You take your most precious commodity—your time—and offer it willingly to another person. A child knows this intuitively and can read between the lines emotionally when promises of time are made and not kept. While kids are super resilient, have a short memory, and are quick to forgive, neglect over long spans of their formative years will take a heavy emotional toll, and if they perceive you don't want to spend time with them, they will receive that information as a message: *I am unlovable.* This perception launches any child into a broken quest for love and validation, making them an easy victim for broken communities of acceptance outside the family. These broken communities of acceptance offer what we are either unwilling to part with or don't know how to give. Always remember that love, in its most universally accepted form, is spelled T-I-M-E in their little hearts.

2. TALK: Asking great questions, hearing and responding to answers eagerly, repeating and commenting on what you hear, and asking follow-up questions is

validating for human beings of any age. Laughing and enjoying the conversation is icing on the cake for a child. Children are born with a natural curiosity concerning their world and are eager to process it with the people closest to them. Smart dads discipline themselves around asking questions to satisfy this hunger to take the world in but also plan time to talk (especially when they are ready to spill their thoughts). Think bedtime dad. Ask about their day. Ask about their highs and lows, peaks and pits, and the things they are looking forward to or loathing. They are ready to talk. Are you?

3. TOUCH: For a child, appropriate physical touch is monumental to emotional and spiritual formation. Think of touch as comfort. How do you feel when you are anxious, hurting in some way, and uncomforted about some issue or situation in your life? God has hardwired human beings to seek out physical comfort. It is as natural as breathing for a child to run to their mom or dad when they are hurt in any way. Reactive comfort must be given physically by dads to their kids. But there is another side to comfort as well—the proactive side. That kind of comfort is unsolicited but spontaneously offered, lavishly bestowed, and for no reason other than that they are yours. This kind of comfort communicates value, belonging, and, above all, love in the most meaningful ways to a child.

A Dangerous Need: Receiving a Strong Blessing

"You are awesome." When we hear those words, it is usually in response to something we did. Not here. Jesus gets a heart-filled, sincere, no-strings-attached blessing from the most important person in His life: "With him I am well pleased."

Once again, it's not because Jesus needs emotional support. He gets it because He's who He is. Every human soul craves this, but in today's self-absorbed social scene there's a limited supply of "just because" blessings based on simply being created in God's image.

A blessing happens when someone offers you any form of approval that allows or helps you to do something. We say, "He blessed me so much that day." Why? Because you needed whatever that person offered in order for some other thing to happen. God's strong blessing of Jesus models for us what people—especially little ones—need so that they can see themselves the way God sees them. Specifically, that they are His masterpieces, custom designed for a unique and powerful purpose. A moment of blessing says . . .

- I approve of who you are.
- I am proud of who you are.
- I see who you are.
- I like who you are.
- You don't need to be anyone else other than who you are.
- Keep doing you!

The dangerous good revolution will be marked by men who bless others and give life with both their words and actions. Big and little spirits are always in need of spoken blessings from a sincere heart. This generation of men is responsible for blessing this generation of children, passing on to others what God has freely lavished on them.

> Praise be to the God and Father of our Lord
> Jesus Christ, who has blessed us in the heavenly
> realms with every spiritual blessing in Christ. For he
> chose us in him before the creation of the world to
> be holy and blameless in his sight. In love he
> predestined us for adoption to sonship through Jesus
> Christ, in accordance with his pleasure and will—
> to the praise of his glorious grace, which he has freely
> given us in the One he loves.[14]

What does Jesus the Son receive from God the Father? What does God want for all His sons to receive? What dangerous needs does God see in children and want to explode into massive blessings through the dangerous good revolution?

Moments, names, love, and blessings.

Dangerous Good Conversation

Think back on your childhood. When did you feel particularly supported by a father figure? What about that memory is so resonant for you?

Can you relate to the powerful parenting God did at Jesus' baptism? Which aspect of that event resonates the most for you? Why?

Time, talk, and touch—which of these is most precious to you? Why? Which do you find most difficult to consistently give to the young people in your life? Why?

What's the first next step for you in powerfully affecting the next generation of dangerous good men?

06

POWERFULLY DELIVERED JUSTICE

Relevancy—Brilliance and Blackness

While women weep, as they do now, I'll fight. While little children go hungry, as they do now, I'll fight. While men go to prison, in and out, in and out, as they do now, I'll fight. While there is a drunkard left, while there is a poor lost girl upon the streets, while there remains one dark soul without the light of God, I'll fight. I'll fight to the very end!

WILLIAM BOOTH

I WAS DAZZLED.

I was twenty-four years old when my dad loaned me money so that I could have enough to buy a stone that, to this day, rests proudly on the left ring finger of my wife. I had never done anything like this before and I was afraid of getting ripped off. This was big. As the jeweler popped the hood of his briefcase, I was expecting to see a small bag holding the diamonds. Instead, he produced a black velvet placemat. After moving the briefcase over to the side, the jeweler slid the placemat directly in front of me and asked, "Are you ready to find the diamond that is going to go on Chrissy's finger?"

No words. My smile said it all. Then, like stars lighting up a jet-black night, he slowly moved the bag from left to right across the black velvet, depositing at least a hundred thousand dollars of brilliant diamonds in front of me. What a showman and what an effect! Against that black velvet I could see every cut and facet of every diamond without struggling.

Without that pad, every diamond would have lost its glory, but with it, each unique stone put forth its own distinct sparkle. This jeweler knew the value of the contrast was necessary for revealing the glory.

As I have traveled the world, I have found God to be somewhat like my jeweler friend. The dark backdrop of our times, broken-male culture itself, and evil on the march worldwide provide the exact contrast a Spirit-empowered movement requires to manifest the glory of God.

The timing and display of the dangerous good to the world is not unlike the journey of the unformed rock that becomes a diamond. Before one finds its setting and place, it is formed in the bowels of the earth by centuries of heat and pressure. Then it is discovered, unearthed, cut, faceted, and polished to shine. Then at last, there is the moment of display against the velvet. The journey is a process.

Continue to work out your salvation with fear and trembling, for it is God who works in you to will and to act in order to fulfill his good purpose.

Do everything without grumbling or arguing, so that you may become blameless and pure, "children of God without fault in a warped and crooked generation." Then you will shine among them like stars in the sky.[1]

Brilliance requires darkness.

Every day, thousands of stories detail the negative outcomes flowing from the beliefs and behaviors of men around the world. Click onto a major news outlet online, and within seconds, you can lament some high-profile politician or celebrity getting caught in a sexual compromise, violence against women, Wall Street greed, or the vulnerable and fatherless young men around the world being swooped into organized crime of all stripes, fomenting violence and terrorizing neighborhoods. The information age has virtually crushed the ability of broken men, male culture, and masculinity worldwide to escape the one thing it has relied on for centuries: staying invisible.

The context of our times is dark, but the dangerous good have been forming through God's process. They are being discovered and unearthed by God's Spirit and are now about to be poured out to shine among the people in neighborhoods, communities, and cities where there is evil, injustice, and hopelessness. According to the statistical experts, there are 2.1 billion Christians in the world. This means that there are between five hundred and seven hundred million "affiliated" Christian men roaming planet earth this very second. And while women of God worldwide are in the church and have illuminated so many lives with their light and presence, the justice and righteousness of God in and through His church will not be possible without the sons of God taking their visible place. For all to see—and for some to hate— the dangerous good, God's diamonds will be spread over the black velvet of injustice on planet earth. Their commission? Shine.

The Resonator and the Relevance

Staying invisible is not an option.

Pain resonates deeply. Any movement that successfully reduces suffering becomes immediately relevant. With the behaviors of men at the center of so much suffering, a movement of men who are dangerous with goodness is both the sign of the Kingdom and the answer to injustice. More importantly, the movement becomes extremely relevant to all people—especially people who do not follow Christ or who are unapologetically antagonistic toward Christianity. Good men doing good things is unequivocally good.

I experienced the relevance of the coming dangerous good movement at a justice conference recently. I had been asked to address community solutions to the mounting issues of orphan care and sex trafficking.

The first speaker was a nationally known expert in human trafficking. She told a moving story of her exposure to the child sex trade in Cambodia. The screen behind her flashed scenes from the very streets she walked, which shook her soul and launched her into a deeper involvement with the justice movement. Her research was the second act. Profound and disturbing statistics about human trafficking locally, nationally, and globally had the audience by the throat. Her last plea to the audience was to not sit idly by but to get involved. I listened closely as she outlined very simple ways people could raise awareness, rescue victims, and rehabilitate those rescued.

The second speaker was the director of an international organization dedicated to helping churches understand and implement orphan-care ministries. Like the first woman, she, too, was over-the-top excellent—articulate, passionate, and well researched. The audience was captivated and so was I, especially when she said, "The orphan epidemic is a symptom of the HIV epidemic in Africa, where whole generations of parents are being wiped out and the children are made vulnerable and left to take care of themselves." Her solution was similar to the first presenter's: raise awareness, rescue the victims, rehabilitate them, and release them healthier back into life.

It was my turn now. I started by saying how much I loved and admired the first two speakers. But then I said, "I have to respectfully disagree with their solutions." You could hear a pin drop.

I went on to carefully explain that we can raise awareness to these issues, we can rescue and restore people, as well as rehabilitate and reintegrate the victims into society. "All of these," I went to say, "need to be done, but these are reactions, *not* solutions."

At this point, my neck was stretched so far out in that room you could have cut off my head with a pair of scissors. So I took a big, deep breath and let it out: "The eight-hundred-pound gorilla in the room when it comes to injustice worldwide is that you can directly trace its origin to the hearts, character, and conduct of men. Truly solving most injustices in our world is like trying to address a massive oil-well disaster in the open ocean. You can skim the surface of the oil spill all day long, feel good about your work, and point to all the oil you have scooped up. But until you cap that well below the surface, it is fantasy to think you have made real progress toward a solution."

I wasn't done with my little rant. "Ninety-nine percent of the energy, investment, and activism is spent on the reaction side to broken-male culture, with no attempts on anyone's part to actually go after the man himself. That is why we desperately need a church-driven social movement that helps men to get into a relationship with God, get healthy as a man, get strong as a believer, and get going into his community. Do that and you take away demand. You deal with the source and deliver hope that goes beyond relief to sustainable generational impact. Do that in combination with the other efforts, then we can begin to use the word *solution*. Helping victims of broken-male culture is not the solution. When the world sees changed men with strong identities who are able to rise above the cultural behaviors producing suffering in the community, *that* will be the time we can truly celebrate."

Something shocking happened that I have never experienced before. The entire auditorium started to spontaneously and continuously applaud. In that moment, I saw both the resonator (stopping pain and suffering) and relevance (Spirit-empowered men turning broken-male culture on its head) of the dangerous good movement. People not only get it but also—and more importantly—long for it to actually happen. In that moment, their hearts suspended all their cynicism, gender bias, and investment in their own "solutions" to the one solution to injustice that makes perfect sense. That moment is the reason you are holding this book in your hands.

[Jesus said,] "A good man brings good things out of the good stored up in him, and an evil man brings evil things out of the evil stored up in him."[2]

Everybody gets *that*.

When a man's character and conduct become healthy, *it changes things*. Most directly, the women and children connected to his life and choices suffer less and develop better. Fewer literal and emotional orphans fall prey to cultural predators who exploit their loneliness, needs, and insecurities for evil purposes. Negative generational and cultural cycles of chaos, dysfunction, and destruction are interrupted. In the crudest analysis, when men have the capacity and power to act in the interests of others versus solely acting in the interest of themselves, the foundational infrastructures of societies and nations improve. Wherever these men go, their characters go with them. Professional, political, social, and religious infrastructures become the beneficiaries of well-formed men; as a consequence, those same organizations become less corrupt and produce fewer cynics.

Women, children, families, communities, cities, and countries could use a few more men like this—men who bring hope by their very presence. Intuitively, people know that spiritually healthy and moral men are like sticks of dynamite: They can create blast zones of life that extend far into the fabric of the society in which they find themselves.

Men are resonating right now and dangerous good men are *very relevant*. They are in high demand but short supply.

Sympathy Not a Substitute for Action

The heart for God is useless without a spine for God.

I asked a church-planting expert who had spent the last twenty-five years planting churches if there were any concerning trends in his field. He said, "We are planting matriarchies" (churches energized mostly by women and children). This admission was a first but not a revelation by any means. It does not mean that men are not affiliated with or attending churches. It *does* mean that, with respect to the energy fueling most local churches, they are functionally or physically absent. Men who may claim the name of Jesus are functionally invisible for Jesus in the larger culture. The dangerous good have now arrived at the harsh reality all male followers of Jesus must confront: *How can it be that there are hundreds of millions of "Christian men" and yet Jesus' church is virtually indistinguishable from the larger culture when it comes to delivering God's justice?*

It's not a stumper.

No spine.

Jesus Christ entered a broken-male culture not unlike the ones that foster so much pain today. He promptly started breaking the rules. He was dangerous with His goodness. He had a spine. He spoke with the Samaritan woman. He had a spine. He told the disciples to let the children come. He had a spine. He defended the woman caught in adultery and stood between her and stones. He had a spine. He touched the physically unacceptable. He had a spine. He touched the ethnically unacceptable. He had a spine. He associated with the morally unacceptable. He had a spine.

For the Son of Man, sympathy and concern for others was not a substitute for *action*. He gave people what they were due—justice. That meant He took up the causes of abandoned women, widows, children, orphans, immigrants, and the poor—classes of people who had no social power and little-to-nonexistent financial capacity, and who were typically exploited. Doing justice was loving and defending those with the least economic, social, or spiritual clout.

Make the connection: The dangerous good are the brothers of Jesus on earth with *this* Spirit of Jesus. They have a heart for God *and* a spine to match.

When Jesus was explaining to His disciples how they would turn heads, He engaged in what would best be described as rhetorical overstatement to make His followers look closely at their own values. It was *deliberate and obvious* exaggeration designed to challenge His followers, address an issue, and make a point. Listen in:

> You have heard that it was said, "Eye for eye, and tooth for tooth." But I tell you, do not resist an evil person. If anyone slaps you on the right cheek, turn to them the other cheek also. And if anyone wants to sue you and take your shirt, hand over your coat as well. If anyone forces you to go one mile, go with them two miles. Give to the one who asks you, and do not turn away from the one who wants to borrow from you.[3]

If listeners take Jesus literally, they will spend their lives codependent, naked, broke, and abused by others! Jesus' words were clearly intended to strike at an issue central to His own life mission, the people He would die for, those who would choose to believe in Him, and the ongoing work of the Holy Spirit in and though Christians: *human selfishness.* It is the same type of hyperbole and exaggeration Jesus uses in the Gospel of Mark when He tells an audience of men to gouge out their eyeballs and cut off their hands in order to get them *to take sin seriously.* He was a master communicator.

His "can't miss" application point in this uncomfortable but forceful exposé on human selfishness is this: Value others in consistent and concrete ways; look for opportunities to be unselfish; and leave "perceived" injustices connected to your efforts in God's hands. *This* is faith in action: trusting Him to use your actions to show His love at work in your life. To be able to act unselfishly in the interest of another is truly a work of God. But to act unselfishly in the midst of an unfair, unjust, and oppressive situation is truly a *witness* to others of His divine power in you. How? Because they *know* you.

This is the import of Jesus referencing going the "second mile." Because taxes didn't pay for all of a soldiers' provisions, they could requisition whatever they needed from conquered peoples. Roman soldiers could require citizens to provide forced labor and were known to abuse the privilege. This issue was a hot button for Jews living under Roman occupation. They would have to stop what they were doing, put their own agendas on hold, and be required to carry a soldier's armor or pack for one mile. Going a "second mile" to serve an oppressor was unthinkable, traitorous, and out of the realm of *natural responses* for every Jew listening to Jesus' words. And that is exactly what Jesus knew they would be thinking when He said those words, providing a perfect backdrop to contrast what His own life, Kingdom service, and Holy Spirit living was all about: *submitting to "unjust" demands and exceeding them for a higher purpose.* The point? Only courageous love, service, and caring will advance the cause.

Jesus' dangerous good followers will not move the Kingdom of God forward without paying a personal price and serving others in ways they would not expect. By doing the unexpected to make *someone else's* load lighter, two things would happen: their attention would be captured and a witness for the gospel would be created. Modeling this kind of "shock service," the disciples would see Jesus serving *them* as they ate, washing *their* feet, fixing *them* breakfast, and, ultimately, dying for *them* on the cross. In the process, He didn't squash their desire for greatness, He simply redefined what courage really is and what it really looks like:

> They began to argue among themselves about
> who would be the greatest among them. Jesus told
> them, "In this world the kings and great men lord it
> over their people, yet they are called 'friends of the
> people.' But among you it will be different. Those
> who are the greatest among you should take the
> lowest rank, and the leader should be like a servant.
> Who is more important, the one who sits at the table
> or the one who serves? The one who sits at the table,
> of course. But not here! For I am among you as one
> who serves."[4]

The Servant King? That's right.

The dangerous good men in the first community of believers succeeded in reproducing the greatness Jesus spoke of by sacrificing themselves for the sake of others. They boldly served the Lord by serving the people: selflessly preaching, teaching, equipping, organizing, and reaching out. Under pressure and persecution, they lightened the load for others spiritually, physically, and materially, trusting God with whatever losses they incurred by going the second mile. A massive audience watched and responded to the different behaviors on display with interest and engagement. Wave after wave of "second milers" were captured, released, and put back into the water stream to do good in unexpected but meaningful ways. The outpouring of the Holy Spirit at Pentecost was an unprecedented earthquake of service and ministry to people that spawned a tsunami of salvation through selflessness and sacrifice.

The first disciples started doing the unexpected in Jesus' name for others. *That* got everybody's attention and became the witness of God in and of itself. Meet the original dangerous good.

> All the believers devoted themselves to the apostles' teaching, and to fellowship, and to sharing in meals (including the Lord's Supper), and to prayer.
>
> A deep sense of awe came over them all, and the apostles performed many miraculous signs and wonders. And all the believers met together in one place and shared everything they had. They sold their property and possessions and shared the money with those in need. They worshiped together at the Temple each day, met in homes for the Lord's Supper, and shared their meals with great joy and generosity—all the while praising God and enjoying the goodwill of all the people. And each day the Lord added to their fellowship those who were being saved.[5]

Just a few weeks earlier, these were the same gorillas jockeying for power among themselves. It was all about them, their titles in heaven, and who would be sitting closest to Jesus. What happened? The Cross and the Holy Spirit happened. What three years of watching the Son of God could not accomplish (driving out the selfish impulse), observing the most courageous act of service and the power behind it did. They watched Him go the second mile and relieve man of his eternal load of guilt and sin by replacing it with Himself. They watched Him love in the midst of oppression. They watched Him not retaliate. They watched Him give up all claim to comfort. They watched Him pay the price to advance the relationship between God and man. They watched Jesus be dangerous with goodness for their sake. They watched Him defeat sin and death. They encountered and experienced the resurrected Christ. They received the promised outpouring of His Spirit. Now on the other side of Jesus' sacrifice, and filled with insight and power, the original dangerous good were on fire to make the same sacrifices for others.

They were now going to be up to no bad.

The Lighteners

Jesus wants to relieve people of their burden.

> Jesus said, "Come to me, all of you who are weary
> and carry heavy burdens, and I will give you rest.

Take my yoke upon you. Let me teach you, because I am humble and gentle at heart, and you will find rest for your souls. For my yoke is easy to bear, and the burden I give you is light."[6]

The mission of the Holy Spirit *in you* is to make this unburdening by Jesus real *in your experience* with Him. The mission of the Holy Spirit *through you* is to make God real to others by you unburdening them in unexpected ways. Unexpected because they are used to seeing and experiencing so much selfishness—or are just used to seeing you! People filled with the Holy Spirit are called to abandon agendas, rights, outrage, resentments, and drop everything when prompted by Him to lighten another's load. This is Jesus, this is the men of the book of Acts, and this is the dangerous good today. Spirit-filled men doing things they never imagined, creating a witness of Christ's work in and through them. In fact, it is so mission critical, Paul the apostle was told by the Holy Spirit to make lightening others' loads a command for every New Testament believer:

Carry each other's burdens, and in this way you will fulfill the law of Christ.[7]

The Holy Spirit is helping sons of the King carry others' burdens in the following ways as they cooperate with Him in the context of their unique lives.

The Dangerous Good Make Others Feel Lighter through Presence

> When we came into Macedonia, we had no rest, but we were harassed at every turn—conflicts on the outside, fears within. But God, who comforts the downcast, comforted us by the coming of Titus, and not only by his coming but also by the comfort you had given him. He told us about your longing for me, your deep sorrow, your ardent concern for me, so that my joy was greater than ever.[8]

Everyday life is heavy! Presence in the midst of heaviness relieves and comforts people. Titus shows up, brings his infectious presence and perspective, and soon the others around him have gone from heavy and harassed to light and delighted. We carry each other's burdens by simply showing up and entering into burdens with others. The pressure gets *redistributed—and sometimes even eliminated—by our very presence.* Someone did this for Titus and now Titus, lighter and freer, is able to get out of his own head and show up for Paul. The Holy Spirit has others in your life and in the community right now who are needing your simple presence to help carry and reallocate the load they are under. The Spirit-empowered man asks: "Are you doing okay?"

The Dangerous Good Make Others Feel Lighter through Providing What's Missing

> All the believers were one in heart and mind. No one claimed that any of their possessions was their own, but they shared everything they had. With great power the apostles continued to testify to the resurrection of the Lord Jesus. And God's grace was so powerfully at work in them all that there were no needy persons among them. For from time to time those who owned land or houses sold them, brought the money from the sales and put it at the apostles' feet, and it was distributed to anyone who had need.[9]

Fill the hole! Spirit-empowered miracles are not fancy. When we see someone burdened by a particular need right in front of us and we have the ability to help meet that need, we provide that which is missing. It arrives on their porch or mailbox, or it is put into their hands.

"Big" opportunities to help rarely come, but the small ones are all around us. When I overheard the audio-video guy in our building was only going to have an orange for his lunch the other day, the Holy Spirit said, *Kenny, go across the street, buy him a burrito, and fill his stomach.* I saluted, got it, came back, and plopped it in front of him. His face was aghast. He said, "Is this for me?" That's the Holy Spirit filling a hole. The dangerous good man is also called to fill emotional holes and spiritual ones too. When you do, you are a lightener in the Spirit of Christ.

The Dangerous Good Make Others Feel Lighter, Presenting Their Needs to God through Prayer

Pray in the Spirit on all occasions with all kinds of prayers and requests. With this in mind, be alert and always keep on praying for all the Lord's people.[10]

Coming alongside and then coming underneath a heavy load many times outstrips our skills and resources. But the Holy Spirit is ready to take on any need and bring it straight to Christ. We don't need to hesitate to bring God's power and peace into a heavy situation through prayer. In fact, transferring burdens to the Lord is the lifestyle the Holy Spirit wants to build in our lives: He lifts our burdens through prayer as we help lift the burdens of others through prayer. When we come into contact with needs *we can't meet*, take them to God with that person. The result? They will feel lighter as someone stronger than they are takes the responsibility for meeting their need.

Do not be anxious about anything, but in every situation, by prayer and petition, with thanksgiving, present your requests to God. And the peace of God, which transcends all understanding, will guard your hearts and your minds in Christ Jesus.[11]

The Dangerous Good Make Others Feel Lighter through Providing Insight

The LORD gives wisdom;
from his mouth come knowledge and understanding.
He holds success in store for the upright,
he is a shield to those whose walk is blameless,
for he guards the course of the just
and protects the way of his faithful ones.
Then you will understand what is right and just
and fair—every good path.[12]

Oil and perfume make the heart glad,
So a man's counsel is sweet to his friend.[13]

In the midst of pressure and heavy circumstances, people's ability to think clearly is almost always clouded. They are too involved emotionally to think simply and rationally. So many think things are fatal and final or, on the other side, wrongly assume everything's going to be okay because then they don't have to accept responsibility for dealing with stuff. In both cases, what people need is someone who can come alongside—without an agenda or conflict of interest—to assess the situation and offer a solution.

So many times, a simple solution eluded me because I was too caught up in the problem emotionally to see it. But then my friend Paul would come along, offer me his unpolluted insight, and my eight-hundred-pound gorilla of a problem would turn back into a hamster. Sometimes the insight feels sensational and other times it demands obedience, but in either case, my heavy load is going to get lighter through godly insight. Paul consciously and actively participates in my life and it is so refreshing in a world that seems to be so self-absorbed (myself included). Sometimes I lose touch with reality and that limits my ability to be a part of the solution for someone else. Paul sees that and so do I, so we've committed to help bring each other clarity in view of the larger mission we have for ourselves in Christ. We don't just want to be associated as friends, we want to be activated brothers who speak words of life for each other when called upon to do so.

> The right word at the right time
>   is like a custom-made piece of jewelry,
> And a wise friend's timely reprimand
>   is like a gold ring slipped on your finger.[14]

The Holy Spirit's words and insight through you to someone else will serve to lift the load they are carrying. This means dangerous good words will be very practical in nature and create real solutions that honor God and people.

An Important Question

When you show up in the lives of others, would they say they feel lighter and more refreshed by being with you or weighed down and burdened?

The dangerous good show up in the lives of others ready to do the unexpected, ready to go the second mile, and ready to pay a price so that burdens can be lifted from others. Sometimes the Holy Spirit will lighten someone's load through you by your presence, redistributing the pressure off one person onto two. On other occasions, He may have you carry a burden by providing what is missing—taking a burrito to the guy across the street or a Ben Franklin out of your wallet. Or sometimes the burden is too big for you or your resources. In those cases, you walk that person to God's porch, ring the doorbell in faith, and enter His house to have dialogue with Him together. They leave feeling lighter and more peaceful knowing He's going to work it out for them *His way* in their best interests. Then, every so often, the Holy Spirit will give you an insight, idea, or angle that their emotions under pressure prevented them from seeing.

Being a "lightener" costs us our selfishness but it gains us brilliance and hope against the darkness. Every Saturday morning, I watch this happen as "Fire Teams" from our church meet to pray and then load into cars in teams of four men to help single parents, widows, the elderly, the chronically disabled, or those who are simply too sick to take care of certain things around the house. On twenty-five blocks around town they show up in their signature shirts, greet their care receiver, get to work for three hours, and leave someone lighter and less burdened when they are done. But before they leave, they always ask whoever they are serving if they can pray for them. This seemingly small act of kindness (to pray for someone) often turns into extended conversations and eternal moments that otherwise would have never happened. People alone in their need are not alone in their need anymore and when all is raked, fixed, repaired, or painted, the prayer time is a sweet theophany, people in the very presence of Christ Himself.

A warning: There is no such thing as second-mile service without meeting our first-mile responsibilities. I see guys all the time pole vaulting over *their* marriage and *their* kids while doing a bunch of service-related ministry or projects outside their homes. The family sees a man who is busy servicing and helping others while his ministry at home is MIA. Remember this, God's man: Your first mile is where you meet the responsibilities already in front of you. The second mile is your *free choice to lighten someone else's load after that*. If you are not married, the same can be applied to honoring your parents, first circle of close friends, or spiritual family. First-mile work *first*. This may cost you your pride, but it will gain you integrity in your second-mile witness.

When Jesus said, "The Son of Man did not come to be served, but to serve,"[15] He was making an identity statement followed by an energy statement, intentionally linking the one with the other. As a man among men, the statement alone made Him stand out in the best of ways and in the most threatening of ways for certain types of men who liked the way things were. In that sense, Jesus made Himself visible through serving God by serving others in a culture where men put a lot of energy into gaining status and position so others could serve them and lighten their load (which was already light because they were born male).

As the dangerous good pursue Christlikeness, the same forces of visibility coupled with the fear of men whose lifestyle we threaten will be manifested. The dangerous good accept the tension that comes with their identity and know how their calling works. Light shines brighter in the darkness. Stars radiate the brightest against the night sky. Diamonds dazzle against black velvet. This is the call to the Spirit-empowered men of this generation.

Shine. Radiate. Dazzle. Serve.

Dangerous Good Conversation

What are the social issues of our time that you find most troubling? Why?

What's the difference between a heart for God and a spine for God? How are the two related?

Why is sympathy not enough? What issues are you sympathetic toward that you could engage in more actively?

What ministry of lightening do you think God might be calling you to? Presence? Providing what's missing? Praying? Providing insight? Where do you think you could contribute in this way?

07

POWERFULLY OPPOSED MOVEMENT

Ferocity—Treachery, Power, and Zeal

—

Those who serve God are the ones who demand Satan's attention, provoke his anger, and call forth his strategies.

E. M. BOUNDS

OUR BIG WHITE VAN WAS LURCHING BACK AND FORTH as we started getting closer to the remote village of San Juan Chamula. We were there to encourage a local pastor attempting to build a church—and to conduct a covert aid and assistance operation to the indigenous Tzotzil (soat-sil) Indian believers. Having left the paved road, we were now amid the squalor and poverty of a rural Mexican countryside. Shacks littered with signs of a hard life and the ubiquitous smell of smoldering fires told us we were not in Laguna Beach anymore, much less the comfort of our hotel many hours away. We were in another world—their world.

We spotted them and they spotted us too. There were no words exchanged, just glares of contempt. I am talking about the local mob bosses—*caciques* (kah-see-kays)—who police these villages with their own brand of frontier justice. There were a dozen or so of them, stopping in their tracks and staring at our large van, searching for clues as to why a load of men they didn't know had suddenly shown up from out of town. What a show of testosterone, complete with white cowboy hats, black alpaca vests, cowboy boots, and burgeoning machismo.

Upon seeing them, our driver appeared unnerved and was sweating, as though he had suddenly caught a bad fever. He was looking at them and at the same time struggling in vain *not to look at them.* Later that day, I learned why: This same group had threatened to kill his dad and told his pop to "never come back" to their town. His dad is a pastor.

Then it hit me, too: I'm a pastor! If the local authorities knew *why* I was there, *who* I was with, and *what I was doing,* there's no telling what their reaction would be. It is widely known that these guys intimidate and kill pastors for sport without conscience or fear of consequences. In fact, one of our visits would include some time with the wife of a pastor who had been murdered recently. Caciques are the judge and jury here, with a low tolerance for those who would threaten traditional ways of living, their monopoly on the economy, or the pagan religious practices they exploit to make money. I think the only thing keeping them from acting hostile toward us was the potential revenue we would bring to their local economy by buying the local crafts (which we did to cover for our true mission).

When our dangerous good unit got out of the van, we saw a massive black statue of a traditionally dressed cacique adorned with a bronze plaque that read "AUTORIDAD MUNICIPALES" (municipal authority). Functionally and culturally it says, "We are the law." Uh, huh, right. That they have to have a bronze statue made to declare it tells the whole story. In my journal that day I wrote:

> What a joke! They don't earn their authority through serving the people; they must manipulate, deceive, kill, and destroy to have influence. Jesus prayed to His Father, "You have given me authority over all men." What Christ must think of such men. We prayed for that day when these posers will meet and surrender to His authority—in this life, hopefully, rather than in the next. Then we went on with our work for a couple hours, then got back into the van to go to our next field of battle.

The dangerous good expect confrontation but keep their eye on the prize. In war, when a group of men are assigned to a frontal assault across open ground or to take a hill, there is a pause *and* a quickening of the warrior. His duty is his alone. The consequences, if he is realistic, are in God's hands. All he knows is that he is getting called into close quarters with the enemy and he needs to discharge his duty to his country, to the cause, and to his comrades. This is the reality of every warrior and of the dangerous good. He knows he is called by

God to combat evil, many times in close quarters, wherever he has been assigned.

The field of battle is not consequential. Whether he is in a remote village in southern Mexico, looking into the eyes of a lost soul in need of care and comfort, or he has a remote in his hand staring at a plasma screen full of porn, he brings himself to *that* battle. He is called to fight *it*, or else he would not have been placed there by God. He would have been taken home already. As long as he is breathing, he is fighting—right where he lives. God's man knows evil is swimming below the waterlines of visible reality. He also is acutely aware that it needs to be called out and driven out by the greater power inside of him.

> Be strong in the Lord and in the strength of His might. Put on the full armor of God, so that you will be able to stand firm against the schemes of the devil. For our struggle is not against flesh and blood, but against the rulers, against the powers, against the world forces of this darkness, against the spiritual forces of wickedness in the heavenly places. Therefore, take up the full armor of God, so that you will be able to resist in the evil day, and having done everything, to stand firm.[1]

The word *struggle* is translated from the Greek word *palē*, which refers to an all-in, hand-to-hand, foot-to-foot wrestling and boxing match. In the first century, wars were not fought remotely with drones or missiles. There was only one kind of fighting—the kind with hands and muscles. In other words, the assumption of the Bible is that the dangerous good will be fighting in close quarters against evil. Human effort is inadequate ("be strong in the Lord and in the strength of his might"), as are human means ("put on the full armor"), if the man in this contest hopes to survive the encounter. Flesh and blood will be the instruments of evil, but "powers," "forces of this darkness," and "forces of wickedness" are the ones we are to attack, grapple with, and subdue through Spirit-empowered prayer. This breed of fighting man is necessary if evil is to be uprooted.

Power threatens power. Men risking spiritually for others threaten men who are rebelling morally. Moral and spiritual courage exposes moral weakness. Men on the wrong side of the equation do not sit idly by as the dangerous good diminish their way of being and gain the admiration of people. History tells us that men with weak ideas who secure respect through fear, control, or violence *will move* to eliminate threats through whatever means necessary. A movement with a moral spine will always be attacked because it exposes how long-held generational or cultural evils lack the ability to give the most basic necessity to people—hope and purpose.

Each year, I take a large group of men from our congregation to Haiti. No amount of training or orientation prepares them for what they will be exposed to or what is about to transpire in their hearts. We visit our three orphanages, which have rescued children from the streets, and before we get out of our convoy vehicle, I say: "When we exit this truck, we are going to light these kids up. We need to match their enthusiasm and energy because they are really excited that you are here. Let's go make their day." We play, swing, laugh, show pictures on our phones, take pictures, pray, and set records for piggyback rides offered and received. They hang all over us, touch our funny (straight) hair, and stare into our eyes with so much feeling and appreciation.

We get back into the truck and motor across the city to a place where 300 adults abandoned on the street have found refuge and, for many, a place to die, thanks to some beautiful Korean nuns. Many have severe physical or mental handicaps, but all of them appreciate a loving touch, a loving prayer, and having their feet rubbed or backs massaged by the men of Crossline Church. They all have a story, there is always a common humanity, and there is always a work of the Spirit in these interactions.

We get back in the truck and pull into a hamlet littered with trash, houses made of tin, tarps, and assorted tree branches. I watch in awe as our men distribute rice, beans, oil, and pasta and then pray over the families who are receiving food. They cry, they thank us in Creole, they raise their hands to heaven, they gladly receive the gospel, and they feel, for that moment, hopeful and not alone because of these Spirit-empowered men entering their need.

These dangerous good men of Crossline tell everyone they meet in Haiti that God has sent them from America so that they could meet. They share their story of faith in Jesus Christ, who is their purpose, and say that He can be their purpose too. For many of my men, this is the first time they lead someone to faith in Jesus and trust the power of the gospel. They are shocked at how attentive, receptive, and ready these souls are to say yes to Jesus through a translator! To feed a stomach is one thing, but to help fill a soul with hope and purpose is a game changer—they have truly become dangerous with goodness in the Spirit of Christ.

This day and this privilege will bring them to exhaustion but, more significantly, to tears.

Briefing the Dangerous Good: "As You Go . . ."

The time of transition had come.

Drafted unexpectedly by Jesus, Peter and Andrew left everything to travel and train with a man who told them that, one day, they would be fishing for men. That conversation by the Sea of Galilee seemed like a distant memory now. They had witnessed Jesus' first message, seen Him reach out to lepers, applaud the faith of a centurion, command a storm, raise a dead girl, make a crippled man walk—and who could forget the power encounter with the demon-possessed man. One word from Jesus' lips and a herd of pigs plunge themselves in to a lake! What a ride it had been.

This whole time, they were learning the way of Spirit-empowered masculinity and how to advance the Kingdom amid hostile men of all persuasions—religious, political, cultural, and Satanic. Jesus was showing them how a compassionate God-man fights during His time on earth, boldly liberating those who were held captive, held down, and controlled by the god of this world and sin.

But now their residency was coming to an end. The season of selection, association, and demonstration was giving way to the next phase: *delegation and supervision.*

The master instructor called a "flight briefing." It went exactly like this:

> Jesus called his twelve disciples to him and gave them authority to drive out impure spirits and to heal every disease and sickness. . . .
>
> "As you go, proclaim this message: 'The kingdom of heaven has come near.' Heal the sick, raise the dead, cleanse those who have leprosy, drive out demons. Freely you have received; freely give. . . .
>
> "I am sending you out like sheep among wolves. Therefore be as shrewd as snakes and as innocent as doves."[2]

That is what you call a green light! Fully empowered by Christ, the very first detachment of the dangerous good were given

- a sanction to fight (approval and authority);
- a message to forward ("proclaim this message");
- targets to find (sick, dead, lepers, demon possessed);

- power to free (to heal, raise, cleanse, and drive out);
- a charge to feel ("freely you have received; freely give");
- a metaphor to familiarize ("sending you out like sheep among wolves"); and
- two commands to fulfill (be shrewd and be innocent).

Jesus didn't sugarcoat it. He gave His seasoned assessment about this campaign to rid the world of Satan's grip through Kingdom advance whenever and wherever possible.

Think "wolves" for a second:

- predatory carnivores that hunt in packs;
- aggressive, greedy, and cruel when they find their prey;
- beautiful to look at but extremely dangerous;
- wicked sense of smell;
- extremely smart; and
- you never want to be caught alone among a pack.

The dangerous good are God's sheep among wolves right now and *you will remain among them* going forward here on earth until you get called back to Christ. One of the main reasons sons of the King are invisible is that we act like sheep among squirrels. There is no enemy to fight, no attacks on the vulnerable, and no need to "get involved." We get along in this world as if there is no hostility.

But Jesus says we are at war with evil for a generation of souls.

We think we know better.

Snakes and Doves

A snake and a dove. Two dissimilar creatures coming together in the disciples for a great purpose.

It's an odd combination, but when Jesus juxtaposes them it starts to make perfect sense. Jesus commanded the Alpha Unit of the dangerous good to be "shrewd as snakes" and "innocent as doves." If the originals were going to be successful individually and as a group, they were going to need great discernment and a pure heart *to transmit* into actions the authority and power they had been given. According to Jesus, wisdom and carefulness (shrewdness) combined with virtue and integrity (innocence) would let them know what to do among the wolves. They were required weapons in the fight against evil and injustice.

A son of the King who is shrewd will

- bring the ax to personal sin;
- guard and protect his faith;
- exercise discernment in all situations impacting his relationships with God and people;
- not allow negative emotions to fester and play into the enemy's plans;
- possess good intelligence on his enemy;
- de-escalate conflict to bring peace;
- sense diversions, distractions, and doubt that cloud issues; and
- act quickly and decisively when needed.

When you think *shrewd*, you think *perceptive* and *not naïve*. What great preparation of his men before sending them into the trenches. In other words, "Be clear and intentional about your mission and don't compromise it by getting lazy." The same command is now put to you as we prepare to go forward into the fight. Jesus is saying to this generation of sons: *Stay sharp, remain on purpose, and don't get sucker-punched by being unwise or impulsive! Be shrewd as a snake and sense the battle on the scales of your spirit, feel the vibrations, and play it smart because to outwit a serpent, you gotta think like one. He's crafty and smart. Don't be out-thought!*

So be shrewd. But add to your shrewdness spiritual innocence. A son of the King who is innocent will

- seek to keep his heart clean so he can hear the voice of God;
- examine himself before God *and* man—no secrets;
- hate evil and run from it if it necessary to preserve his integrity;
- keep polluting influences from corrupting his relationship with God;
- soak his mind in God's thoughts through daily reflection in His Word;
- seek aggressive accountability and utilize it to win his battles with evil; and
- serve and help others with unselfish and eternal motives.

Jesus knew that innocence to evil and sin would provide maximum clarity of mind and reception to His Spirit in battle. Compromises of the mind and heart would create interrupting static that hinders the effective communication necessary when fighting both seen and unseen evils. Imagine a radio man on the battle line who is unable to call in mortar rounds because his cable has been cut or his signal is jammed. This is the picture. Personal purity of mind, body, and devotion insures higher battlefield acuity and ability to hear the Spirit of Christ among the wolves. Innocence to evil, according to Jesus, means more impact in the fight against it.

Jesus is calling the dangerous good to prepare our spirits. As a community of men, our personal commitments to train in wisdom and commit to spiritual integrity are critical. Our King always demanded the real deal: "Why do you call me, 'Lord, Lord,' and do not do what I say?"[3] To fight with Jesus means to be all-in, hands stacked on His, eyes locked, and agreed that we will take this fight to the last breath—no shortcuts. Versus what? Half-in, with the keys to the back door in your pocket in case things get uncomfortable. He also desired His dangerous good to *actively defer to and be directed by* divine wisdom and realities over their own. That's why He prayed over us, "Sanctify them by the truth; your word is truth."[4] A spiritually shrewd and innocent man is a man of the Word.

Lastly, Jesus told us that there would be a direct link between our personal purity of heart and our ability to experience God's presence: "Blessed are the pure in heart, for they will see God."[5] On the battlefield, you need good communication, hand signals, and collective intuition as a team. This kind of nonverbal and spontaneous communication is life and breath to a fighting unit amid suppression fire, grenades going off, and blood being spilled. Spiritual integrity and innocence to evil take one worrisome individual out of play—you! It lets you rise above the noise and tune out Satan's temptations and manipulations designed to distract or divert you from securing others' well-being.

Passion is not enough. According to Jesus, shrewdness and innocence are required. Why? Because Satan's experience and treachery will defeat spiritual immaturity and zeal every time. The evidence is all around us—God's men who are flashes in the pan and don't finish strong because they underestimated Satan, didn't account for opposition, and didn't believe evil truly existed. But when real wisdom and purity are applied to the fight and then combined with your zeal for Christ, unstoppable men and a movement advance.

Mr. Wolf, meet Mr. Snake-Dove and his friends—otherwise known as the dangerous good.

Blowback and Comebacks

Blowback is the unintended and adverse results of an action taken. Julius Caesar's famous words "Et tu, Brute?" resonates the shock and awe of an attack he never dreamed would happen. "Even you, Brutus!" Caesar said to his best friend, as his longtime ally drove the knife deep into his flesh.

If Satan can't get you to retreat from becoming like Christ and bringing God's love and justice to others, there are plenty of other unwitting soldiers available for him to use that you least expect. As you press into becoming like Christ, start connecting with your brothers, initiate delivering help and hope in tangible ways, and people see you doing it—watch your back. This is one of the devil's most twisted and effective forms of discouragement.

"Let's see," he reasons. "I want to annihilate the church, attack the glory of God, and strike a blow against God's Son. Got it! I can kill three birds with one stone by sowing discord and division within God's people as their unhealed fears and unconfronted pride permits. If I can get them fighting among themselves, becoming analytical, discontent, competitive, and selfish in their perspectives toward their brothers, they will be my agents." Study the New Testament closely and you see that Christians have a propensity to exchange their newfound freedom in Christ to lift up believers for another agenda—an evil one.

> You, my brothers and sisters, were called to be
> free. But do not use your freedom to indulge the
> flesh; rather, serve one another humbly in love.
> For the entire law is fulfilled in keeping this one
> command: "Love your neighbor as yourself." If you
> bite and devour each other, watch out or you will
> be destroyed by each other.[6]

The issue being addressed is believer-on-believer behavior. A sure sign Satan has hijacked a heart is a self-righteous and critical spirit of a Christian toward other Christians. Something tragic and sinister has happened: The Holy Spirit has been replaced by another spirit in the name of religion. Some Christian's self-made standard has been breached, the Spirit of Christ has been fired, and there is a new, self-appointed deputy practicing character assassination in the name of God. Martin Luther King Jr. was right: "We must all learn to live together as brothers or we will all perish together as fools."[7] Satan is highly invested in the perishing part. But the Bible says that sons of the King counter such accusation and division by keeping our eyes on the ball: Serve people in love. That means you attach less to what people say, more to what God says, and let God deal with nitpickers on that day when all men will give account. "It is not the critic who counts," Teddy Roosevelt said. "The credit belongs to the man who is actually in the arena."[8] Going forward, the dangerous good concern themselves with mission, not mouths. Just don't be surprised. It's called blowback—the unintended results of good actions taken.

> Dear friends, do not be surprised at the fiery
> ordeal that has come on you to test you, as though
> something strange were happening to you. But
> rejoice inasmuch as you participate in the sufferings
> of Christ, so that you may be overjoyed when his
> glory is revealed. If you are insulted because of

the name of Christ, you are blessed, for the Spirit of glory and of God rests on you. If you suffer, it should not be as a murderer or thief or any other kind of criminal, or even as a meddler. However, if you suffer as a Christian, do not be ashamed, but praise God that you bear that name.[9]

Open hostility in enemy territory is not unusual; it's to be expected. The world systems under Satan's control drive their respective cultures or governments to openly persecute Christians. Persecution comes to those upon whom "the Spirit of glory and of God rests." Did you catch that? Uncooperative Christians don't require persecution because they are already blending in nicely with the culture around them. Without a word, the actions of the dangerous good say it all as they shine the light of Christ in a world that rejects Him.

Persecution, while openly hostile toward Christians, is also the most counterproductive tactic for Satan. As believers don't cave into it, God is glorified. As believers suffer for their faith, they are made even stronger. As nonbelievers and believers alike see Christ demonstrating His power in and through persecuted believers, people see there is a cause worth giving your life to that transcends all earthly powers. Numbers go up. Study the waves of persecution in the first and second century. The church exploded. More recently, study the evolution and powerful character of believers forged in the fire of communist persecution in China. According to Open Doors International, there are presently more evangelical Christians in China (more than 97 million) than there are in the United States.[10] My own encounters with the persecuted Tzotzil Indians of southern Mexico bear out the same principle—they act like they have already won and are fearless.

The dangerous good will be called to suffer, but whatever form it takes only fuels us. We prepare for it, expect it, thank God for it, face it, remain focused on eternity, and ask God to use it for His purposes. We are not promised escape or deliverance. We are promised, however, that any suffering experienced for the sake of Christ will bring a revelation of Jesus Christ to those who witness it. In the end, persecution gets stuffed back in Satan's face: "For we who are alive are always being given over to death for Jesus' sake, so that his life may also be revealed in our mortal body."[11]

The Bible is clear: Satan has today's cultural, political, and toxic religious systems under his influence and he uses these instruments to exact his vengeance against God by bringing persecution to God's people. The dangerous good will be catching flack in the days to come, but remember, it's exactly because you are a son being molded into the image of the Son who risked it all for you. What Jesus modeled for us is meant for us.

The dangerous good have internalized something that other men have not: *Taking risks for God leads to a richer relationship with God.* More importantly, we know that when we push the envelope of His promises, we get to personally see His purposes and power manifested in the world in real time. As you consider the potential blowback for being aggressive with Christlike compassion and goodness among the wolves in today's culture, remember this:

Do not throw away your confidence; it will be richly rewarded.
You need to persevere so that when you have done the will of God, you will receive what he has promised. For,

"In just a little while,
he who is coming will come
and will not delay."

And,

"But my righteous one will live by faith.
And I take no pleasure
in the one who shrinks back."

But we do not belong to those who shrink back and are destroyed, but to those who have faith and are saved.[12]

Here is your guarantee and your charge. Your faith account will be settled in your favor as you risk dangerous goodness among the wolves. Further, God promises you will be elated with your reward. But the investment must be made now. The caciques of this world have many different forms, but the dangerous good always meet the blowback with this promise and find their power: "All authority in heaven and on earth has been given to me."[13]

No regrets in the end means no retreat now.

Dangerous Good Conversation

—

Who are the caciques in your world today? What are some ways you could stand up to them in your day-to-day life?

Do you tend more toward dovelike innocence or are you naturally more serpentine? What helps you to honor both commands from Jesus?

What type of blowback makes you the most nervous? How can your dangerous good brothers help you keep courage in the face of it?

08

POWERFULLY REMEMBERED MEN

Visibility—the Song of the Unsung

—

Deeds will not be less valiant because they are unpraised.

ARAGORN FROM J. R. R. TOLKIEN'S *THE RETURN OF THE KING*

SOME PEOPLE ARE KNOWN FOR BEING WELL-KNOWN.

In today's entertainment culture, Jimmy Fallon is one of my favorites. To borrow his own lingo, he is "so great" as the host of *The Tonight Show* and the champion of late-night television. Just to test his visibility, I did a spontaneous poll of our Southern California congregation during a message: "How many of you know who Jimmy Fallon is?" More than 99 percent of those present raised their hands with great affection and energy.

Then I asked: "How many of you know who Alicia Swanson is?" Not one hand, no affection, and no energy.

Alicia Swanson is my older sister. Living in Sacramento,

California, she is separated from Jimmy Fallon and New York City by 2,800 miles, straight across the country along Interstate 80.

Having anticipated both responses, I labeled Jimmy a loved celebrity and my sister a loved hero and then contrasted the main differences between those two types of people. Jimmy versus Alicia looked like this:

- Celebrities are known for their name being known. Heroes are known for thinking of someone else.
- Celebrities show it's possible to be wildly famous. Heroes show it's possible to be dangerously good.
- Celebrities make history through visibility. Heroes make history through noble qualities.
- Time passes and dissolves a person's celebrity. Time passes, creates space for hindsight, and reveals true heroes more clearly.

We prize having heroes—those among us who do things that are selfless or sacrificial, putting others' needs before their own. Some are known in their lifetime for their exploits, while others remain invisible in their time and become appreciably visible only *after* they are dead and gone. We call these men and women "unsung heroes" because they never received any recognition while they were still living. Most families have unsung heroes in their ranks—moms, dads, brothers, sisters, aunts, uncles, grandparents, and so on. My unsung family hero is Alicia, who received a phone call from my seventh-grade English teacher, Mrs. Mueller, asking her to tutor her little brother, who was flunking all his classes. It's not normal for a seventeen-year-old sister to set aside extended portions of her social life to be her brother's personal tutor without major pushback, complaining, or both. Yet that is exactly what Alicia did in the winter and spring of her senior year of high school. With the clarity only hindsight provides, I see that this year of my life was when my trajectory took a turn for the good—because of my unsung hero:

- I made honor roll that last quarter of my seventh-grade year and then all four quarters of my eighth-grade year, securing at least four As and two Bs each grading period.
- I entered my freshman year of high school feeling confident and performed well enough all four years to apply and be admitted to the University of California Los Angeles (UCLA) upon graduation.
- I met my wife, Chrissy, at UCLA while leading a Bible study, and after her graduation, we married, started a life together, and raised three awesome millennials.
- My experience at UCLA introduced me to Campus Crusade for Christ, and after graduation, I became a staff member in full-time ministry.
- My experiences in ministry motivated me to pursue a career in behavioral health and put me on a path to becoming the CEO of a healthcare company specializing in mental health.

- Seeing the connection between faith, family issues, and men during my healthcare years, I started to research and write books addressing men's issues. You are reading book number twenty-three.
- I have circled the globe more than one hundred times to share the Good News of Jesus, and God has chosen to use this one-time failing seventh grader to discuss being God's man with millions of men.
- That exciting and challenging journey has led me to help energize a movement—which I've called the Dangerous Good—of God among men in this generation.

Thanks for saying yes to Mrs. Mueller, Alicia.

Unfortunately, words are one-dimensional, and you can't feel what I feel as I reflect on an amazing journey that is not yet over. God used my unsung sister to change my trajectory away from dropping out of school and redirected it toward education, Jesus, and a life of helping people. When I bring it up with her, Alicia deflects the attention away from herself and minimizes the place of importance she owns in my heart. As much as I love Jimmy Fallon (whom the world knows), he can't touch my big sister (whom you likely didn't know until this chapter) in the hero department. She is the one who worked behind the scenes in my life, the one who no one ever saw, not caring that someone else got the credit.

It's mind blowing to boil your whole life's trajectory down

to one person's decision to be unselfish in a moment in time, but that is the power of the unsung hero.

The Bible is full of unsung heroes and behind-the-scenes people making small decisions to be dangerous with goodness that result in eternal blast zones they never could have predicted. For your sake, I am glad they are visible enough for us to see, learn from, and imitate, because they represent the majority of men who form the dangerous good movement. We will be in the mix of humanity, making huge differences via small-yet-powerful decisions for Jesus in the right spaces.

Luke, the author of the Acts of the Apostles, took great pains to highlight one of the greatest "unsung" people in the Bible—Barnabas. He is a second act to the disciples, the apostle Paul, and the writers of the New Testament, but without his willingness to enter others' lives, historic Christianity would have unfolded much differently than we know it today. This is the journey of the dangerous good—not thinking about how we will be perceived now but entering others' lives as God's Spirit leads and leaving the results (and the impression we leave) to Him.

History and heaven sing the songs of the unsung.

Barnabas: The Song of the Willing

Greatness starts with willingness.

For a dangerous good man, to be willing means to be prepared to cooperate with God's Spirit, to do God's will *without* being asked. Read that again. That's Barnabas. This is a playlist of his songs as sung by history and heaven. These tracks are Spirit-filled, very dangerous, and will leave you wanting to be like him.

Track One: A Willingness to See and Lift Up Others

All the believers were one in heart and mind. No one claimed that any of their possessions was their own, but they shared everything they had. With great power the apostles continued to testify to the resurrection of the Lord Jesus. And God's grace was so powerfully at work in them all that there were no needy persons among them. For from time to time those who owned land or houses sold them, brought the money from the sales and put it at the apostles' feet, and it was distributed to anyone who had need.

Joseph, a Levite from Cyprus, whom the apostles called Barnabas (which means "son of encouragement"), sold a field he owned and brought the money and put it at the apostles' feet.[1]

Three things characterize the first community of Spirit-filled believers: uncommon attitudes, uncommon actions, and an uncommon corporate unity of life and purpose. Within this ocean of blessing and power among God's people, one man's unsung attitudes and actions caught Luke's attention: a guy named Joseph from Cyprus, who, because of his nature and actions, picked up the nickname "Barnabas" from the disciples. What did this man do to pick up the label "son of encouragement"? What consistent, defining actions or familiar behaviors prompted them to dub him Mr. Encouragement? Picture, for a moment, the discussions when Joseph/Barnabas was not around:

- "That Barnabas is so considerate of others."
- "Do you know what Barnabas did for me totally out of the blue?"
- "That Barnabas is so supportive."
- "When you talk to Barnabas, you feel like you are the only person on the planet."
- "Did you hear what Barnabas did with his land? You won't believe it."

This man voluntarily *filled others* with courage, hope, strength, faith, and perspective that lifted them up emotionally. This is the definition of an encourager. His brothers *felt something from him*, and they loved what they felt! But none of those good feelings and connections happen without a man being willing to set himself aside at any moment in order to see and lift up others. Encouragers enter lives and fill them with something that people can't conjure on their own. Barnabas definitely had this gift and used it frequently enough to earn him this nickname from his brothers. Whether you are naturally inclined to encourage or need to develop the discipline, know this: To bring encouragement into the lives of others is to be dangerous with goodness.

We have different gifts, according to the grace
given to each of us. If your gift is prophesying, then
prophesy in accordance with your faith; if it is
serving, then serve; if it is teaching, then teach; if it
is to encourage, then give encouragement.[2]

The current culture of digital self-absorption and living
in the "connected" age of technology has, by default, created
a famine of personal encouragement. A screen cannot see;
it cannot give the kind of feedback required by a human
being created with a soul needing nourishment. To this end,
God has stacked the deck for this generation of the sons
of encouragement—setting a stage for their light to shine.
Humanity is so overly connected to their "un-life-giving"
screens that when a real, life-giving encourager sees, enters,
and starts lifting them up, they feel something positive.

Called by Christ to bring encouragement, the dangerous good are on patrol in the normal spaces of life, starting
with the people God has placed in close proximity: people
who live with you, people who work with you, people next
door, people who play on a team with you, people you coach,
believers who fellowship with you, and the person who serves
up your morning coffee every day. No need to dance around
the edges or dip your toe in to gauge the temperature; this
water is perfectly warm. Assume those around you are defi-
cient when it comes to being personally encouraged. Dive in
like Barnabas.

Christ's dangerous good should be the most encouraging

men found anywhere on earth. An ongoing relationship with Jesus Christ is so powerfully encouraging that what's happening inside should naturally translate to what's happening on the outside—your actions toward others. It starts with how God has strongly encouraged His sons.

> May our Lord Jesus Christ himself and God our Father, who loved us and by his grace gave us eternal encouragement and good hope, encourage your hearts and strengthen you in every good deed and word.[3]

Under-encouraged people cannot be awesome encouragers. By contrast, unexpectedly, wonderfully, and overwhelmingly encouraged people have the experiential responsibility to give away what they now possess. The dangerous good are the recipients of eternal encouragement through Jesus Christ's actions. We were once without hope, stuck in sin, separated from God, and hustled by the world, flesh, and the devil when it comes to our identity and our purpose. Jesus enters the picture, demonstrates His love for us on a cross, and proceeds to deliver forgiveness, redemption, our truest identity, and real estate in heaven. The result: We step into a life eternally secured by His love and the peace of His promise. This is the most encouraging thing that can ever happen to someone.

But here's the problem: Even those who have been super-encouraged by God can forget just how encouraging God has been to them. They become dry in God and wet with self-absorption, making them virtually indistinguishable from the unredeemed.

This is why we have Communion, why we gather with other believers, why we are called to remind each other, and why we must daily have our noses in God's love letter to us—the Bible. God has given us these disciplines, avenues of worship, fellowship, and discipleship to restock our soul with His encouragement. "Do this in remembrance of me,"[4] Jesus told His dangerous good. He wants us to be in the habit of remembering His sacrifice, personalizing it, and internalizing afresh just how loved and eternally blessed we are by God. This is the close, intimate, and eternal connection that separates the dangerous good from other men and makes them consistent and Christlike encouragers.

> God did not appoint us to suffer wrath but to receive
> salvation through our Lord Jesus Christ. He died for
> us so that, whether we are awake or asleep, we may
> live together with him. Therefore encourage one
> another and build each other up, just as in fact you
> are doing.[5]

Through the gospel and His servant Barnabas, God is saying to this generation of His sons, *Listen up. In our family, we encourage people.* But what if we fail in that commission that is so close to God's heart? What if we fail to remember, replenish, and release Spirit-filled encouragement to others?

The Bible tells us exactly what will happen: "You may be hardened by sin's deceitfulness."[6]

God says that without encouragement, the human soul goes from soft and open to hard and deceived. It is made that way by its environment, by intentional neglect, or by simple lack of exposure to living water or shade. Think about a flower bed left unwatered for days during a heat wave. The soil, the predictor of growth and life, is baked, brittle, and has no moisture to nourish the plant's roots. God tells us that the hot and searing sun of ambivalence, disconnectedness, and self-absorption bakes and hardens a soul unwatered by encouragement. A hard coating forms over people's minds, which isolates them and makes worse any part of their life that is broken, selfish, discontent, cynical, or skeptical. Without life-giving encouragement, over time, people will begin to believe lies like

- "This is just who you are and always will be."
- "You will never have a breakthrough."
- "God doesn't care about you."
- "You can't rely on anyone but yourself."
- "Who would want you?"
- "You don't have anything to offer."
- "Why bother? Just end it."

The devil is thriving in today's desert of discouragement because it is easier to lie into the hearts of the discouraged than into those who are lifted up and filled up. To this end,

God has stacked the deck for the dangerous good to shine the light of Christ.

Somewhere in his journey, Barnabas realized that encouragement cost him so little but meant so much to others. That's called an easy win. The world is waiting for the unsung heroes of Christ to sing the song of Barnabas: To be dangerous with goodness means receiving God's salvation and encouragement and then being willing, right now, to see and lift up others in advance of God asking you to do it. We know hearts are open. Now—eyes open!

Track Two: A Willingness to Take the Road Less Traveled

When he came to Jerusalem, he [Saul] tried to
join the disciples, but they were all afraid of him,
not believing that he really was a disciple. But
Barnabas took him and brought him to the apostles.
He told them how Saul on his journey had seen the
Lord and that the Lord had spoken to him, and how
in Damascus he had preached fearlessly in the name
of Jesus. So Saul stayed with them and moved about
freely in Jerusalem, speaking boldly in the name of
the Lord.[7]

Saul's reputation—before his infamous encounter with the resurrected Christ, he had persecuted Christians—was a problem. People simply could not accept another narrative from a man who had been so energetic, passionate, and brutal in his pursuit of Jesus followers in the region. So while Saul (later Paul the apostle) recounted his testimony of dramatic conversion until his voice gave out, it didn't matter. He had a label that shut down all discussion. Imagine what that was like for Saul as he was now obedient to what God had called him to do!

Number one on his to-do list was to get the approval and endorsement of the first elders of the church. For an early leader in the church, it would be like having your passport stamped at the border in order to explore a country: no stamp, no entry. This is exactly what happened to Saul, and the only stamp he got was: REJECTED.

Enter Barnabas.

Did you catch it? "They were all afraid . . . [b]ut Barnabas . . ." Luke observed. Barnabas heard about what happened, saw Saul, and promptly marched him back into the headquarters of the Jerusalem council, where the passport stampers were meeting. Everybody else was running away from Saul; Barnabas was going toward him. The gossip and sentiment about Saul were strong, but the faith of Barnabas was equally resolved. Knowing that he was Saul's best and only chance, Barnabas decided to help a brother and secure for Saul what he could not secure for himself: acceptance.

I wish I could have been there when Barnabas approached Saul. I imagine it like this:

"I knew this would happen," Saul is saying to himself. "God, what is going on? What's the matter with these people? I came all this way and for what, Lord? Who do they think they are?"

Just as he is about to let out some colorful words for ox dung, he hears these words: "Hey. You're Saul, right? I was there in Damascus. Come with me."

A man he does not recognize and knows little to nothing about is motioning him back to the direction of his latest and most profound disappointment. Saul has no clue about Barnabas's clout. Poor guy. What a way to meet your new best friend. You walk in hopeful. You walk out rejected. You walk in a second time with Barnabas.

Barnabas marches Saul right into the middle of the action with all his reputation and relational leverage for the purpose of getting Saul appointed to ministry. All the questions about Saul evaporate in the next few minutes, and he walks out of "command and control" with the full endorsement of the council. That's a God wink—His unmistakable hand doing unbelievable things.

This unsung hero of history has, by taking a road no one would travel, changed history. He could never know the full impact of this moment, either before or during his intervention to save Saul from falling through the cracks.

Going down the road less traveled has massive historical relevance for the dangerous good:

- Saul obtains the Jerusalem council stamp of approval, which gives him both the authority and freedom he needs to preach the gospel anywhere Christians exist.
- He can plant churches wherever he evangelizes and wins people to Christ.

- He can pastor, advise, equip, and encourage those same churches through letters.
- Thirteen of the twenty-seven books of the New Testament written by Paul are rooted in this moment.
- One of those books (Romans) inspires Martin Luther's spiritual breakthrough, spawning the Protestant Reformation, which changes Western civilization forever.

All of us need a champion sometimes. All of us struggle. All of us feel lonely. All of us can come under clouds of sadness and isolation, which obscure our ability to see God's purposes for our lives. All of us have been the new person at one time or another. Without meaningful connection, even the most passionate believers, like Saul, can return to old ways and old patterns if they are not made to feel included and encouraged in their calling.

Thank God for the "Barnabases" of the world who break rank, doing and saying something different from what the group is doing or saying, all for the sake of those whom God has sent them to for that reason. That is the purpose of this community—to be disruptive in a healthy way, in the Spirit of Christ, and to stand with and for others.

Being willing to take the road less traveled is not an event or an aberration; according to Christ, it is our lifestyle:

Enter through the narrow gate. For wide is the gate and broad is the road that leads to destruction, and many enter through it. But small is the gate and narrow the road that leads to life, and only a few find it.[8]

Whoever wants to save their life will lose it, but whoever loses their life for me and for the gospel will save it.[9]

Jesus is upfront: The life of faith involves regular experiences of tension—pulling and letting go so that you can serve God's purposes. Dangerous good behavior is Spirit-empowered behavior that is counterintuitive to a watching world. It's show stopping: Just when they expect you to do the self-protective thing, you do a Spirit-filled thing out of love for God and people. You take the road less traveled, and the tension inside of you releases itself into faithfulness to Christ for the sake of another.

Be ready, like Christ and like your brother Barnabas, to put on your blinker.

Track Three: A Willingness to Submit to the Holy Spirit's Control

News of this reached the church in Jerusalem, and they sent Barnabas to Antioch. When he arrived and saw what the grace of God had done, he was glad and encouraged them all to remain true to the Lord with all their hearts. He was a good man, full of the

Holy Spirit and faith, and a great number of people were brought to the Lord.[10]

The news was historic: REVIVAL HITS THE GREEKS!

As Jesus predicted, Peter prophesied (at Pentecost), and the Jewish prophets foretold, God's family was expanding into the world of the Gentiles through Christ. The elders in Jerusalem heard the report and moved quickly to verify it with some "boots on the ground" intelligence. But whom would they send?

Answer: Mr. Encouragement—the man who sees and lifts up people. The man who will go down the roads less traveled. The man who is filled with, controlled by, and led by the Holy Spirit.

Prior to His departure, Jesus told His dangerous good followers how the relationship would work after He returned to heaven:

> I will ask the Father, and he will give you another
> advocate to help you and be with you forever—
> the Spirit of truth. The world cannot accept
> him, because it neither sees him nor knows him. But
> you know him, for he lives with you and will be in
> you. I will not leave you as orphans; I will come
> to you.[11]

Jesus said, "My leadership in your life and your entire Christian experience will transition and then rest upon your conscious connection with My Spirit in you." While strange to hear at first, any confusion the first community of dangerous good had regarding the Spirit of Christ living within them had given way to an experiential clarity and power. This is the journey every follower of Christ takes. That is how a relationship with Jesus is set up to work: His Spirit in us, leading, guiding, and speaking His will to our spirit.

This connection to Jesus' leadership through the Holy Spirit was conspicuously obvious to Luke (the writer of Acts) as he observed Barnabas. This unsung hero and giant in God's Kingdom possessed a close connection to the Spirit of Christ, which had been poured into his heart upon belief. It was also a huge reason he was selected to shepherd, encourage, and cultivate this new group of believers. He was known for saying yes to the Holy Spirit's control, which, consequentially meant he was fully prepared for any and every situation that God called him to enter.

Like Barnabas, dangerous good men are full of the Holy Spirit. It doesn't matter how you arrive at your place of filling. You can arrive there logically, as in "He's God, I'm not; He says it, and that settles it." Or you can arrive there out of the pain of trying to live the self-sufficient and dry Christian life, as in: "I don't want to rely on my own power anymore; I want to live for Christ." The most important thing to God is this: Once you are informed and commanded to be filled, you are responsible to act. Let's get informed so we—like Barnabas—can be used by God in powerful ways to care for others.

It starts with the command to be filled.

Do not be foolish, but understand what the Lord's
will is. Do not get drunk on wine, which leads
to debauchery. Instead, be filled with the Spirit,
speaking to one another with psalms, hymns, and
songs from the Spirit. Sing and make music from
your heart to the Lord, always giving thanks to God
the Father for everything, in the name of our Lord
Jesus Christ.[12]

When the dangerous good man says yes to the filling of the
Holy Spirit, it is important to remember that the decision—
by default—is a no as well. Any time we say yes to the Holy
Spirit's control, we are saying no to self-management, cultural norms, impulse, and the devil. We surrender total control of the decision-making to the Spirit of Christ inside and
obey the Voice within telling us to do what will show love for
God or people in a moment in time.

The image of being filled with the Holy Spirit is a familiar
one but with a twist—being drunk. You know a person is
drunk because the "spirit" they have ingested is taking over
their words and actions in a sloppy and uncontrolled way.
The Bible draws on what most men have seen, known, or
experienced themselves to help us make sense of our experience of being filled with (ingesting) the Holy Spirit. Your
behavior will be taken over by Jesus! We drink deep, we drink
long, we get filled with and controlled by the Holy Spirit.

This was Barnabas and this is us. God's word is crystal clear: *Be filled with the Holy Spirit.*

Consider yourself informed or reinformed. Now, a fair question is, How is living your life "filled" with the Holy Spirit going?

- Have you said yes to the Holy Spirit's control and asked Him to fill you today?
- Have you been acting under your own control or His control today?
- Have you been self-sufficient or humbly dependent on and listening to Him today?
- Have you been fighting His voice in your life today?
- Have you been listening to other voices today?

It may come as good news to you (it does for me) that all dangerous good believers must ask themselves these questions on a regular basis! It is also comforting to know that if you get derailed in your connection to the Holy Spirit, you can get back on track by simply transitioning control back (from yourself, other influences, or lies) to Him. Because Jesus instructs us to be in close contact and partnership with the Holy Spirit, the dangerous good do it eagerly, expectantly, and, above all, *willingly.* Here's an example of a prayer willingly placing oneself under the control and direction of the Holy Spirit:

> Holy Spirit, I need You. I know I am tempted to be
> in control of my life, and when I am, I miss out on

Your work in and through me. I am sorry for taking over control when I shouldn't. Thank You for Your continuous presence and willingness to direct my life. I ask, Holy Spirit, that You take control of my life right now and fill me. Lead me, guide me, speak to me, open my eyes to what You want me to do, and help me choose that today, moment by moment. Thank You for taking control and filling me. In Jesus' name. Amen.

Don't be afraid—God's cheering you on and saying, "Drink up!" He wants to see His Spirit take over your thoughts and actions in a dangerously good and godly way. Go direct and go now.

Fill up. Suit up. Then show up to encourage.

Track Four: A Willingness to Offer Others a Second Chance

Some time later Paul said to Barnabas, "Let us go back and visit the believers in all the towns where we preached the word of the Lord and see how they are doing." Barnabas wanted to take John, also called Mark, with them, but Paul did not think it wise to take him, because he had deserted them in Pamphylia and had not continued with them in the work. They had such a sharp disagreement that they parted company. Barnabas took Mark and sailed for Cyprus, but Paul chose Silas and left, commended by the believers to the grace of the Lord. He went through Syria and Cilicia, strengthening the churches.[13]

Bailing out in the middle of a mission doesn't sit well with most men—especially the people who were depending on you. As you read about the heated exchange above, you can imagine Mark's feelings of shame and embarrassment when his past failure is the source of a massive argument between two dangerous good giants. It's like when MMA champion Conor McGregor fought boxing great Floyd Mayweather Jr.—it was shockingly good and it went on longer than anyone expected. While the Bible doesn't give details, it tells us enough when it relays, "They had such a sharp disagreement that they parted company." They literally incited and provoked each other to the point where they could not even talk to each other. Ever been there with someone?

Imagine you are Mark watching all this go down. Barnabas believes the best in him and is willing to give him a second chance, to the point where he is willing to choose Mark over Paul. Remember, this is the same Barnabas who got Saul's (now Paul) passport stamped. Not the prettiest vignette in the Bible, but the story isn't over:

- God overrules the disagreement for the good—instead of one missionary expedition, there were now two!
- Paul later acknowledges Mark's worth in his letters to the Colossians and Timothy.

- Peter acknowledges Mark's ongoing participation in the movement in his first letter.
- Mark goes on to pen one of the four Gospels approved and accepted by the early church fathers as written by the Holy Spirit.

The power of a second chance! No wonder Peter and Mark later became such good friends! At some point, they both felt that God could not use them again. Yet both were met amid sadness over their mistakes, offered a second chance, accepted it, and powerfully served Christ as dangerous good "re-recruits."

Perhaps as you are reading these words you are asking yourself: Is this for me? Is Jesus re-recruiting me? The answer is a resounding *yes*! You are the unsung hero of this movement whom God sees and wants to use in a new way to bless your generation. The Spirit of Christ in Barnabas who championed Mark's second chance is the same Spirit of Christ who gives men today their second chances.

We all need second chances. We also need to take full advantage of those second chances. Wherever you fit in that spectrum, God is calling forth and calling back all His unsung heroes into Jesus' mission.

There is work to do that only you can do.

The dangerous good generation will change the worlds of millions in the days and years to come. Spirals of blessing will unfold out of unsung moments of decision that no one will see but God. Wave after wave after wave of God's providential goodness will cascade forth, covering the globe in ways the initiators will never know and could not possibly fathom. And yet the song of God's unsung heroes on earth will eventually be sung. It's God's nature to see His boys doing good.

> God is not unjust; he will not forget your work and the love you have shown him as you have helped his people and continue to help them.[14]

Knowing this reality fuels the dangerous good as we prepare our hearts to reach out. We are not looking to man but to God as we decide to be the man He sees, remembers, and rewards at the time of His choosing. The first community of the dangerous good provides us with models, mentors, and messengers, known and unknown, visible like Saul and behind-the-scenes like Barnabas.

As such, we are eager to be the "valiant unsung"; that is the authentic nature we seek for our community today. Dangerous decisions that some may see will be made by Spirit-empowered men, but the vast majority of interactions will happen in smaller spaces and are destined to remain anonymous to most men. The cast of characters and acts of the dangerous good will mirror very closely the Acts of the Apostles in form and spirit—a few visible catalysts to be sure (the apostles), but the majority of the movement will be a forceful wave of the valiant unsung.

God is pressing play on your unsung song.

Dangerous Good Conversation

—

Who are some of your unsung heroes? Why are they heroes to you? How might you honor them this week?

How comfortable are you with the thought of being "unsung"? How can you guard against the temptation toward celebrity or self-praise?

How are you most like Barnabas? Do you see and lift up others? Do you take the road less traveled? Do you submit regularly to the Holy Spirit? Do you offer forgiveness and second chances to your brothers?

What's one aspect of Barnabas's heroism that you could work on for yourself? What's the first next step for you to take?

09

POWERFULLY IMPASSIONED MEN

Fervency—the Arrival of Revival

—

The story of Christian reformation, revival, and renaissance underscores that the darkest hour is often just before the dawn, so we should always be people of hope and prayer, not gloom and defeatism. God the Holy Spirit can turn the situation around in five minutes.

OS GUINNESS

A MAN'S TRUEST PASSIONS PRODUCE HIS TRUEST PRAYERS. My surfer friend prays for the arrival of the perfect swell, along with the ability to judge a wave, catch it, stand up quickly, cut it neat, and ride it clean and strong. My snowboarding community is a simpler lot—we simply pray for fresh oceans of powder to carve. My fellow golfers pray for putts that lead to birdies, which lead to scores under par. Most singles pray for "their person" to spend the rest of their life with. Brides with outdoor weddings pray for good weather. When I was growing up, my mom played bingo; a serious (20 cards at a time) player, she asked me to pray for "her numbers" to be called in vertical or horizontal patterns.

You get the picture. We pray for things that we expect will provide the satisfaction we seek. Whether you think these prayers are frivolous or legitimate, make no mistake—they always are fervent. Passions have hopes, hopes have prizes, and prizes produce prayers because *the outcome we want isn't totally within our power to secure.*

So we pray.

This simple, authentic connection between true passions and our truest prayers has great significance for those in whom a radical and transcendent love for Jesus Christ has taken root. The first community of the dangerous good was a praying community and their prayers reflected pressing and desperate desires that God honored. What was their deepest desire they felt would bring them the greatest satisfaction as followers of Jesus? What did they want more than anything? Just as surfers ask for the arrival of waves and snowboarders ask for the arrival of powder, men passionate about Jesus began asking for the arrival of revival.

This connection of passion for Jesus and prayer for revival is the only thing standing between the dangerous good and a worldwide movement of God's Spirit among men again. It is not a matter of technique, organization, or form—it is a wild fire of the Spirit that becomes uncontainable. It is expressed in prayer and lived under aggressively until what is sought is secured. In a prophetic jump across time and space, what has been modeled for us by the first community of the dangerous good is now meant for this generation of Spirit-empowered men. It is straightforward, is not a matter of talking, and *has everything to do with power.*

The Kingdom of God is here.

When Desires Collide

It's called collision theory. When the right particles or molecules collide, they create a chemical reaction, manifesting in what is called *activation energy.* Think of dough rising: That is activation energy arising out of a simple collision. Yeast collides with and feeds off simple sugars, resulting in the release of carbon dioxide and alcohol. As the carbon dioxide and alcohol escape, the bread rises. Chemists would say that sugar and yeast are "suitable particles," because when they collide, you can count on energy being produced. You can't see this chemical process with the naked eye, but you know that something is going on because the dough is now puffier, taller, and starting to look more like a roll or loaf of bread. In its crudest form, a loaf of bread is really the result of a successful collision of particles and the impact of the energy flowing out of that impact. People worldwide (including me) are very grateful for this collision!

So what do suitable particles, chemical reactions, and activation have to do with the dangerous good revolution? By now you might have surmised the answer, but I will say it anyway: everything.

When the desires of the dangerous good to see the greater

works of Jesus collide with the mission of the Holy Spirit in the world, the result is revival. More specifically, revival is the activation energy emanating from that divine chemical reaction to men desiring the works of God *to happen among them* and the Holy Spirit wanting to work among those men. As we see it in the Bible, as we see it in church history, and as it is coming about right now, the dangerous good movement will experience four things:

- God touching and transforming the hearts of individual men on a large scale;
- God manifesting His power in the communities of men *gathering* around His purposes worldwide;
- God extending His power to transform the wider society through the witness and harvest of Kingdom rule in each epicenter; and
- God creating movements everywhere where every man knows some man who is a committed follower of Jesus Christ.

Men will start to rise, and while you can't see the Source of it, all present will know God's Kingdom power is at work because

- lost people are being saved;
- prodigals are recommitting their lives to Christ;
- marriages are being healed, restored, and reconciled;
- believers are spiritually growing into maturity and as servants of Christ;

- hurting people are being encouraged and finding joy;
- people in bondage and addiction are being set free in Christ;
- the least of these are being served;
- believers are serving with their gifts;
- leaders are being reproduced and spiritual multiplication is accelerating;
- believers are increasing their stewardship and giving generously;
- people are praying and prayers are being answered; and
- laborers are being called and sent out by the Holy Spirit into the worldwide harvest.

This collision produces some serious earthly and eternal fireworks. The environment is one of people pursuing Christ and being radically changed by the power of the Holy Spirit. The environment is not of talk, social-media postings, political ideology driven by CNN or Fox News, or boutique activism. King Jesus and His called subjects are entering His realm of existence, power, and purpose together in front of a watching world. The question is not: "Does the Holy Spirit want to work in me in dangerously good ways?" He is ready and waiting. The more pressing issue is: "Do you want God?"

Heaven and earth need to collide.

In the 1700s, George Whitfield, Charles Wesley, and their dangerous good friends wanted God's works among them, and their desire precipitated a collision of epic proportions. The result was the Great Awakening in colonial America and the formation of bands—groups of men dedicated to God, each other, and advancing God's purposes.

In the 1800s, Charles Spurgeon and his community of common men wanted what the Spirit wanted and prayed for a "rushing mighty wind" versus a soft breeze of the Holy Spirit.[1] The result was the subsequent salvation and baptism of more than fourteen thousand people at the Metropolitan Baptist Tabernacle over the next thirty-one years.

In the 1900s, William Seymour called on men around him, men who—like Frank Bartleman—wanted to see the greater works of God in their midst. The entire region of Southern California experienced the Azusa Street Revival birthed in Los Angeles. Black men, Hispanic men, white men, their women, and their children prayed and sang together, creating a radical Kingdom unity unprecedented for their context. So unusual was the mixture of blacks and whites that Bartleman enthusiastically told a local newspaper, "The color line has been washed away in the Blood"![2]

The common denominators in all these movements? Spirit-empowered men wanting God, and the Holy Spirit wanting to work among men, colliding for revival. The beauty and power of these dangerous good men is that they were common jars of clay holding an uncommon passion, along with a willingness to show up to their calling without regard to the opinions of men. The need for professional ministers and preaching comes to an end and is replaced by Kingdom life coming, changing and transforming men by Christ's power. Spurgeon himself saw it:

If we had the Spirit sealing our ministry with power, it would signify very little about talent. Men might be poor and uneducated, their words might be broken and ungrammatical; but if the might of the Spirit attended them, the humblest evangelist would be more successful than the most learned divine, or the most eloquent of preachers.[3]

Desires collide and power flows, "sealing" the movement, guiding common men, and showing forth Kingdom power over man's abilities. Activation energy is released and men start rising up and shining the light of Christ.

Dangerously Wanting God

What do I do? This is what most men ask. We want to move through the process as efficiently as possible to get to the desired outcome. We agree with the goal and say to whoever is leading or training us, "Let's do this!" Gather and go, right?

Well, sort of. There isn't an app for this but, fortunately for your group of Christ-seeking friends, there is a very good road map and model to follow in the first community of believers. Their experience and expression not only answers the question about where to put energy but also directs the dangerous good into the results the Holy Spirit desires. More than any other moment in this conversation, what follows will make or break the Holy Spirit's goal of dangerous good movements everywhere, where every man knows some man who is a committed follower of Jesus. With Scripture as our lamp and the new community of Christ followers in the book of Acts as our most trusted guides, we will ask: *What do we see people doing because they want God?* We will let that lifestyle of revival speak to us individually, guide us as groups of men, and steer us to accelerate the mission of the local church. Finally, we will "pull the bus over," stop, and really focus on how to pray for revival in a dangerous way.

First things first: What first actions and investments of their time and energy did the first community of believers give to God so that He could multiply them into the salvation and transformation of so many?

Called Together

They devoted themselves to the apostles' teaching and to fellowship, to the breaking of bread and to prayer. Everyone was filled with awe at the many wonders and signs performed by the apostles. All the believers were together and had everything in common. They sold property and possessions to give to anyone who had need. Every day they continued to meet together in the temple courts. They broke bread in their homes and ate together with glad and sincere hearts, praising God and enjoying the favor of all the people. And the Lord added to their number daily those who were being saved.[4]

For their part, the first community of believers did the following things, which accelerated revival:

- Gathered together
- Grew together in God's Word
- Prayed together
- Shared life together
- Did church together (Temple courts)
- Did smaller groups together (homes)
- Worshiped together

Key word? *Together.*

The first community of Christ followers believed that the greater works Jesus had promised would happen if they were together seeking it in these specific ways. This is a challenge in the digital-consumer age, which by its very nature is highly individualized, detached and screen based, easily diverted, and tailored to the needs of individuals. The quality of community depends on a unifying larger purpose and focused togetherness, and a customized, individualistic culture impacts the nature and substance of what *together* means.

But for the first followers of Jesus, being together was a calling and the oxygen that made life in God both possible and powerful for aggressive Kingdom advance. This is why we see, here and in subsequent revivals across church history, a commitment to meeting, seeking God, and asking the Holy Spirit to come and minister to them in a *new way.* What that new way looks like will be outlined a little later.

But what you need to know for now is that revival involves *newness versus oldness.*

When asked why His men didn't pray the way all the other religious guys of His time prayed, Jesus said this:

> No one sews a patch of unshrunk cloth on an old
> garment, for the patch will pull away from the
> garment, making the tear worse. Neither do people
> pour new wine into old wineskins. If they do, the
> skins will burst; the wine will run out and the
> wineskins will be ruined. No, they pour new wine
> into new wineskins, and both are preserved.[5]

Fresh versus used is the theme here. Jesus is clear: The old way will break under the force of this new collision between man's desires and His works. So we can't just do the same old, same old.

The first community of followers wanted God *in a new and different way* and they would pursue it together.

Between "Together"

> One day Peter and John were going up to the
> temple at the time of prayer—at three in the
> afternoon. Now a man who was lame from birth was
> being carried to the temple gate called Beautiful,
> where he was put every day to beg from those going
> into the temple courts. When he saw Peter and

John about to enter, he asked them for money. Peter looked straight at him, as did John. Then Peter said, "Look at us!" So the man gave them his attention, expecting to get something from them.

Then Peter said, "Silver or gold I do not have, but what I do have I give you. In the name of Jesus Christ of Nazareth, walk." Taking him by the right hand, he helped him up, and instantly the man's feet and ankles became strong. He jumped to his feet and began to walk. Then he went with them into the temple courts, walking and jumping, and praising God. When all the people saw him walking and praising God, they recognized him as the same man who used to sit begging at the temple gate called Beautiful, and they were filled with wonder and amazement at what had happened to him.[6]

Peter and John are on their way to church when they are "interrupted." They are not with a big group of believers. They are not at church. They are not in a home group. They are not at a prayer meeting or Bible study. As revival unfolds in real time, we see two dangerous good men doing what men who desire the greater works of Jesus do—amid humanity and *between* being together. Specifically, we see them

- SEIZING OPPORTUNITIES God presents to minister when apart from one another;

- GIVING JESUS AWAY when apart from one another; and
- TAKING RISKS for Jesus when apart from one another.

This is the essence of revival's outward expression—risking for Jesus in the open when God calls you into contact with others "on the way." The first community of the dangerous good were connecting and then separating, but whether they were together or apart, they were taking strong steps of faith in an effort to see the greater works Jesus had predicted come about. In the larger picture, this willingness to actively engage organic ministry opportunities amid the everyday needs and struggles of humanity unlocks an even greater collision of Spirit and movement. Power attracts.

Peter and John heal the beggar and, like a fist fight on a playground, people zoom to the spot, gossiping and gawking. Seeing the numbers and prompted by the Spirit, Peter does what people who want God do: He seizes the moment, gives Jesus away, and takes a huge risk for the gospel by preaching a Kingdom message of faith and repentance. The result? Two thousand more believers. Peter is feeding [Jesus'] lambs.

The religious establishment is witnessing this out-of-control, dangerous, and accelerating wildfire of Spirit-empowered men who care. They become afraid and competitive. In this Spirit-empowered movement, God chooses not to use religious professionals, which, by default, threatens, offends, and creates enemies. To add insult to injury, God is using regular, peanut-butter-and-jelly guys with no seminary degrees but who are filled with, led by, and sensitive to the promptings of the Spirit. This "simply will not do" for the professional class, who "know better," so they have God's dangerous good arrested. "Greatly disturbed"[7] is how Luke describes their fear mixed with arrogance.

What do you do when dangerous good power threatens man's power? Listen to a loaded question and Peter's response:

> They had Peter and John brought before them and began to question them: "By what power or what name did you do this?"
>
> Then Peter, filled with the Holy Spirit, said to them: "Rulers and elders of the people! If we are being called to account today for an act of kindness shown to a man who was lame and are being asked how he was healed, then know this, you and all the people of Israel: It is by the name of Jesus Christ of Nazareth, whom you crucified but whom God raised from the dead, that this man stands before you healed. Jesus is
>
> 'the stone you builders rejected,
> which has become the cornerstone.'
>
> Salvation is found in no one else, for there is no other name under heaven given to mankind by which we must be saved."[8]

This is a drop-the-mic moment two thousand years before anybody ever publicly dropped the mic. There is no greater triumph than the triumph of the truth—especially the truth of the gospel. Unable to dispute the lame man's healing, the religious authorities warn the dangerous good and tell them to "shut it." Unfortunately for them, in doing that they just threw more gas on the fire. And that leads us to the next thing that men who want God and a collision with the Holy Spirit do.

Reporting His Story

> On their release, Peter and John went back to their own people and reported all that the chief priests and the elders had said to them. When they heard this, they raised their voices together in prayer to God.[9]

This last event in the story completes the rhythm of the first community of the dangerous good in a physical and practical sense. They are hungry to be together and pursue Him together in specific, intentional ways. Then they separate to do life, shine the light of Christ in their context, and pursue His greater works. Finally, they come back together again to share what God is doing in their midst. Naturally, this reunion provokes praise and prayer before the cycle supernaturally repeats itself. It is a community saturated in God and in His works. Together under the Holy Spirit.

Apart working with the Holy Spirit. Together again under the Holy Spirit.

Press repeat.

The Prayer for Power

True God encounters drive the truest praying.

Millions of people pray, gather, worship, study the Bible, and share spiritual life in community around the world, but few pockets of these activities are awakening God's people to their true nature and purpose in the Kingdom of God. And yet, God wants to do exactly that using the dangerous good movement of Christlike men.

There is prayer that feels like a gentle breeze or a fine hand shake, and then there is prayer that sounds and feels like a mighty wind and throws you crashing into the King's realm and work. These prayers are unmistakable and come from the deep well of strong desires. They pulse with a base of power flowing from simple integrity, simple words, and strong motives to see God's hand move immediately, if possible.

Upon hearing how God has used Peter and John to shine the light of Christ, glorify God, and hold forth the gospel under pressure, there is a spontaneous eruption of prayer.

> "Sovereign Lord," [the disciples] said, "you made the heavens and the earth and the sea, and everything in them. You spoke by the Holy Spirit through the mouth of your servant, our father David:

'Why do the nations rage
and the peoples plot in vain?
The kings of the earth rise up
and the rulers band together
against the Lord
and against his anointed one.'

Indeed Herod and Pontius Pilate met together
with the Gentiles and the people of Israel in
this city to conspire against your holy servant
Jesus, whom you anointed. They did what your
power and will had decided beforehand should
happen. Now, Lord, consider their threats and
enable your servants to speak your word with
great boldness. Stretch out your hand to heal and
perform signs and wonders through the name of
your holy servant Jesus."[10]

If we want to realize the hope of this generation, we must
have hearts like this that utter prayers like this that reap
responses like this from God. And while God cannot ever
be reduced to a formula or manipulated or held hostage by
anything we say or do, there is a clear backbone to this prayer
of revival that the dangerous good can seek to reproduce
with our own hearts before Almighty God. People wanting
a revolution of the Spirit among them pray like this and
God has given us this prayer intentionally as a model for our

community in this hour. This is how people who want to see the greater works of Jesus manifested in their midst pray. They don't go small.

Dangerous Praying Affirms What's True about God

Sovereign Lord recognizes that I am talking to the One who is totally capable and ready to do whatever He pleases any time, any place, and in any form He chooses. God is fully in charge of everything connected to our context, our community of believers, and our experiences in the community, both good and bad. He is *over* all things, *bigger* than anything we can see, and *willing* to sovereignly intervene in any circumstance.

You made the heavens and the earth and the sea acknowledges that the person we are talking to is the Creator who calls into being things that did not previously exist. He doesn't need a wand or a spell or even a drum roll. He simply thinks it. As such, He is not limited by any circumstance or human limitation.

They [Pilate and Herod] did what your power and will had decided beforehand should happen confesses the reality of God's authority over man. He is controlling every aspect of the story. Kings, rulers, authorities, governments, bosses, generals, or overseers of any kind all operate under the supervision and scripting of God. Confusing as that is at times, His higher purposes are always being worked out—as was the case with Peter here. God decided he and John would be seized because He wanted them to be given a platform and audience to testify and a great story of deliverance to report, which would spark this prayer.

Dangerous Praying Comes Against Opponents of the Gospel

Now Lord, consider their threats admits that you can't do anything about antagonists, but God certainly can! The axis of evil included Pilate, Herod, and their hidden inspirer, master planner, and thwarter of all things connected to Christ and the building of His church—the devil. As we have mentioned, revival and the Kingdom of God are not about talking but about true power that saves, changes, and transforms lives. That kind of power threatens power. Dangerous praying acknowledges the real enemy and asks God to contend and eliminate all threats to the gospel.

Dangerous Praying Asks God to Manifest His Unmistakable Power

The final aspect of dangerous praying is calling for some serious close-air support for the infantry and the mother of all Holy Spirit bombs to be dropped. They want shock and awe so that there is no mistaking who is behind the events they are asking for—and it's not them!

> Now, Lord, consider their threats and enable
> your servants to speak your word with great
> boldness. Stretch out your hand to heal and perform
> signs and wonders through the name of your holy
> servant Jesus.

As brave as this is, it is the most dangerous of all aspects of this prayer for God's cause and greater works to go forward. When God answers this request regarding His cause and His glory, it will make life for the disciples even more uncomfortable and combative. It's not about them and they know it.

Key words: *your hand.* Asking God to "stretch out" His hand takes the credit for any miracle away from any disciple who, because of pride, wants others to see God use them versus see God alone. The dangerous good delight in God's power, not because He uses them to display it. The request has others and their thought processes in mind—a power event that is exclusive to them ministers more deeply, touches more personally, and argues more soundly for Jesus and the gospel than human words or means. Where words and reason do not work, God can and will do whatever it takes to glorify Himself and advance the gospel of His Son.

Power speaks louder than words.

The Kingdom Comers

After they prayed, the place where they were meeting was shaken. And they were all filled with the Holy Spirit and spoke the word of God boldly.

All the believers were one in heart and mind. No one claimed that any of their possessions was their own, but they shared everything they had. With great power the apostles continued to testify to the resurrection of the Lord Jesus. And God's grace was so powerfully at work in them all."[11]

God hears the prayers of His dangerous good and thinks, *Earthquake. Perfect way to let them know I am listening.* Seriously. He's the sovereign Lord and the Creator who can call anything into being: anywhere, at any time, in any way. While the Bible doesn't give the extent of the shaking, God gives His people an earthquake so they will unequivocally know that He is pleased with this prayer and these hearts. He knew what was coming and that they were going to need unshakeable faith. So, God fist-bumps His dangerous good.

Empowerment follows, and they receive the boldness they asked for. Boldness plus generosity plus unity between them would validate their call and their fellowship to the end.

This is a bold community who asks for more boldness because Christ has purified their passions, reformed their hopes, and replaced worldly prizes with eternal ones. Notice the order of this first community as a road map for the dangerous good: God first, people second, and material things a distant third. Walls—economic, racial, social, and spiritual—coming down is a witness of Kingdom rule. People were more important than things. Mess that up and you have neither God's response nor God's revival.

With boldness comes more comfort with being uncomfortable for Christ. When men accept the call of Jesus, they also accept the knot that following Him sometimes puts in their belly.

The road to revival among men starts in your own heart. Our truest passions produce our truest prayers. What do you want?

- Do you want to see the greater works of Jesus done in and through your life as He promised?
- Do you want God to touch the people you love and the community you live in with His power?
- Do you want God to visit and shake your community of believers?
- Do you want to see lost people saved, believers filled and empowered by the Holy Spirit, and the Kingdom of God to come upon your life?
- Do you want to be dangerous with goodness like King Jesus?

If those are your desires, start talking to God, gathering with your brothers, growing spiritually with your brothers, and praying with your brothers, and be ready to act with your brothers when God visits you with the power of His Spirit. The church in this hour must have men who believe it is their identity and their duty to be dangerous with goodness in the image and character of King Jesus. It is time for your truest passions to produce your truest prayers so you can live your truest life.

You're open to an earthquake, right?

Dangerous Good Conversation

—

When was the last time the Holy Spirit answered your passionate prayer with an earthquake? Share a memory of a seminal moment of prayer from your life.

How do you react to the idea that the passion of the dangerous good will invite opposition? What gives you courage to keep moving forward?

What do you want God to do next in your life? In your church? In your community?

10

POWERFULLY CALLED
FORWARD

Bravery—Understanding the Times

The most critical need of the church at this moment is men, bold men,
free men. The church must seek, in prayer and much humility, the coming
again of men made of the stuff of which prophets and martyrs are made.

A. W. TOZER

YOU LIVE IN PROPHETIC TIMES.

Percolating underneath your world as you know it today, real existential threats are lurking *that have to be confronted.* Real women and children in besieged cities and communities are suffering. Real orphans, real sexual slaves, real fatherlessness, real domestic violence, and real death are being displayed nightly on all our screens in all places around the globe all at once! Thanks to digital technology, it's now almost impossible to look away. These clear and present sufferings spawn real fears that are metastasizing and diluting personal courage among us. At the same time, they are creating a vacuum the wolves among us want to exploit.

The phenomena we all see and sense on our screens can be rightly called "history in the making." You will either be part of the problem or part of the solution, for good or for evil—but a moral blank you cannot be. This is your first step forward.

There is no visible social movement purposed to confront the ills brought on by lesser men, merciless masculinity, and the unsavory thugs who enjoy all the suffering they cause. Gotham is in trouble but Batman will not save us. Batman is a myth but our need is real. People are desperate for help, but who will come? Who will make things better? Who will bring justice? Who will give the bullies a taste of their own medicine?

One thing we know for sure: It's up to us. We know that reactions and protests address the evils of our times from the outside in, which, by its very nature, is doomed to failure and, in fact, has failed. Problems never exist only at the level at which you see them; but an "outside in" perspective will keep reacting to the symptoms while never addressing the roots of the dilemma. Neither will salvation come from the shallow waters of celebrity cult, overhyped media movements, and identity politics. They are all paper tigers without fangs that cannot stop a thing. Culture is recognizing it needs a movement of good men exactly because what's out there now is noise, not real progress.

The third sign we are living in ominous spiritual times is the ever-growing assault on the differences between men and women, which leaves every form of traditional masculinity vulnerable to a blitzkrieg of criticism and a call for reformation. Neutering men of their God-given inner wiring and natural strengths is not the answer. My grave concern in this environment is for my millennial brothers.

The public outcry we see in our world today is to simply purge society of the broken "alpha male" and its equally broken thinking and behaviors. Unfortunately, "alpha male" is the caricature all men find themselves lumped in with or having to distance themselves from in order to avoid the crosshairs of a demonstration. Worldwide, guys remain committed to self-preservation, self-indulgence, and self-importance at the expense of others in their lives. The word *self* is always inextricably linked to the suffering of others.

What are you to do in the midst of all these perceptions? Go forward.

Breaking Through the Line

A group of guys with their backs to the wall have three options:

1. Surrender—wave the white flag and capitulate. Neither glory nor honor there. May be pragmatic, but it's a nothing burger for the masculine soul.
2. Fight to the death—you're going to die anyway, so go down swinging. Glory and honor there but you are out of the fight completely and permanently, and you don't get to see the fruits of the bigger fight.

3. Break through—muster numbers, pick a spot in the battle line, charge hard at it, break through, and then regroup to be a part of the bigger victory in the days to come.

Whatever the reason you picked up this book, I am praying to God that, going forward, you are ready to break through all forces that oppose your identity and expression of Christlikeness in your generation. We are fully aware that the news is bad out there, the horizon is dark, and we are talking about one mad dash against a wildfire of spiritual and cultural opposition. But one thing I know from traveling around the world speaking to millions of men is this: *Buried in the ashes of cultural confusion are strong embers of goodness.* They're there. There are also millions upon millions of us who are done choking on the bad news of our times. Loud, large, and consistent pounding sounds of a movement are being struck in the hidden refineries of masculinity worldwide. Strong winds created by desperate times are fanning the resolve of men into a fighting spirit that is dangerously and energetically good. It is the stuff of war—it is a back-to-the-wall, no-escaping-this-moment, unavoidable clash with evil within and without that will define this generation of men.

So if you ever wondered what you would do if evil was on your doorstep, wonder no more. That moment is here. That moment is upon you. A decision from deep inside must be made. Good men know in the recesses of their minds that the truest and best defense against the dark parts of broken-male culture is a powerful incarnation of spirit through men manifested in strong actions, courageous compassion, and sacrificial love.

Just as there have been painful ideological uprisings and movements of men dominating the news cycle, an equally strong, Spirit-empowered, and relationally driven moral dynamic is invading men's hearts across the globe. This new, growing spirit among men worldwide makes a powerful case that there is an upside to healthy male culture.

Jesus told His disciples that men could belong to culture (the world) or belong to Him. He then proceeded to tell them He had "chosen" them out of culture and brought them intentionally into His community. He knew both communities were available to men and that both would have their own impact. One would produce pain. The other would reduce it. One would bring hopelessness. The other would bring hope.

This idea of communities of men who believe their purpose is to be aggressively good in their time on earth resonates deeply and is relevant to all on the receiving end of that goodness. What do you call movements everywhere of men who have decided to answer the bell of history and come out of their corner ready to fight for such an unexpected revolution of masculinity? What do you call a wave of men who meet the demand for life-givers versus destroyers, blessings to humanity versus curses, redeemers versus villains?

They are called the dangerous good.

Without fail, every revolution of good is composed of

those whose blood is boiling and heart is breaking at the same time. I am praying for both of those to happen right now in you.

The dangerous good revolution will be composed of those men who have had an inner and Spirit-empowered wake-up call so powerful that it takes over their purpose for the rest of their lives. Men from diverse backgrounds, ethnicities, and cultures will have this spirit in common. These ordinary men who are living in this extraordinary moment of history will be remembered for one thing—they rose up and fought the good fight with their brothers. They understood the heart-beat behind Burke's observation I placed at the beginning of our discussion: "When bad men combine, the good must associate; else they will fall, one by one, an unpitied sacrifice in a contemptible struggle."

Being connected to the dangerous good means that being known as a "good guy" is not enough. You recognize that the "good guy" label is a defensive and selfish posture that is sought after so that you don't get lumped in with the thugs, the jerks, and the tools of this generation. It's safe, but it's also a waste of energy—it benefits nobody but yourself. Dangerous good, on the other hand, is proactive, other centered, and aggressive in the best of ways. It's a spiritual aggression that has its eyes on a higher prize—taking territory back from evil in your world.

It's exciting to be a part of something so big, powerful, and positive. It's also a worthy thing to help redirect the discussion about men in the public arena away from one universal caricature to one that reflects a meaningful social expression of good.

I have tried to stress the Kingdom dimension to everything because this movement can't be a rah-rah speech. When you have studied men's movement history like I have, a picture emerges: *a lot of inspiration but not a lot of meaningful community to foster real progress and impact.* Trust me— I was there. Inspiration is meaningless without a real, *ongoing* commitment to connect with other Spirit-empowered men.

That is why I am making no assumptions based on past men's movements and the prospect of you becoming a part of the dangerous good. Going forward, allow your own heart, your own prayers, your own common sense, and your own conscience to be your frontline voices to the masculine direction presented here. It is imperative that this generation of men approach morality and the spiritual mission against evil with a somewhat blank canvas. Every man who has taken in these pages will have had some identity formation—good or bad. But we have to define this road map very clearly. What we have discussed, informed primarily by God's Word, should shape what dangerous good means internally, in our friendships, in our posture toward women, in our relationship to our children, and with our neighbors. Only when we see clearly how relevant the dangerous good movement is for them will it become relevant to the larger culture and world we seek to impact positively in the days ahead.

We're living in a new age of masculinity that, ironically, requires the best of traditional male culture while jettisoning the thinking and behaviors that caused so many women and children to suffer. The men of this generation have both a massive opportunity and the daunting challenge of picking up the slack for decades of broken-male culture at every level of society. The self-serving features of the alpha male have been rejected and should stay rejected. The over-soft and sensitive features of "omega male" created by feminism is now annoying to women and is not serving women and children very well. The hunt is on for a new blend of tough and tender, committed but compassionate, relational and rugged, ready to sacrifice but also ready to serve. So as evil presses in, planet earth, secular society, and the man on the street are all being forced to directly and indirectly ask the truly seminal question of our times: *Where have all the good men gone?* I wouldn't have believed that possible until I read that exact headline on the front page of the *Wall Street Journal*. You must see, the dangerous good are in high demand but very low supply.

And, finally, a warning. You are living in a time when gender activists are striving to create a cultural consensus: that masculinity itself is harmful and should be replaced with a more fluid version that is less oppressive, less selfish, less domineering, and less, well, masculine. It is my prayer that the dangerous good movement of Spirit-empowered men will make the case that we don't need to neuter men of their inherent drives, natural strengths, or physical tendencies—that is simply energy. The solution (versus the reaction) would be to foster and support any movement that successfully produces men of character whereby that character results in conduct that serves versus abuses people and humanity. What the advocates of social re-engineering are forgetting is that while men who have power and influence but lack character make the negative headlines, there are millions of men who are strong but possesses good character who, by their unity and aggressive goodness, will become visible. As the dangerous good, we call this phenomenon of our movement "shining the light of Christ."

Because things that become visible get noticed and examined, expect energetic pushback somewhere along the way. *The pushback tells you that you are right on track!* I recently read that a men's conference trying to help men become better husbands and dads was protested because it was "men only."[1] These are the times we live in. But when you see where this energy is coming from, you'll know why it's there. It's because you are moving successfully against evil and providing a living illustration of Kingdom community that will be attractive and strong to most people. History bears witness to the power of persevering in moving forward and eternity will confirm it: Martin Luther King, Abraham Lincoln, William Wilberforce, and many of the believing men who, knowing they were risking their lives, signed the Declaration of Independence. The world was ready, the brave were called, and they banded together to do what was right before God and man, driving revolutions of good and standing up to injustice. Like you, those men I just mentioned, along with their called brothers and sisters, went against comfort and the cultural tide to become the dangerous good of their time.

It's your time now.

Dangerous Good Conversation

—

When was the last time you felt like your back was against the wall? Did you surrender? Fight to the death? Break through?

Who are the men in your life you can muster to join God's dangerous good battle against evil?

What first next step might you and your dangerous good friends take?

NOTES

INTRODUCTION: POWERFULLY MADE: GLORY—THE DANGEROUS GOOD IMPULSE

1. Luke 4:18-19, NASB; also see Isaiah 61:1-3.
2. Galatians 4:6, NASB
3. Romans 8:29
4. Matthew 4:1-11
5. Matthew 4:4
6. Ecclesiastes 3:11, NLT

01: POWERFULLY FORMED MEN: IDENTITY—THE LOST LIONS

1. Jeremiah 4:3-4, NASB
2. John 4:34
3. 1 Timothy 6:11-12
4. 2 Peter 1:12-13, NASB
5. Mark 12:14
6. Matthew 11:19
7. John 9:4
8. Matthew 25:21
9. John 17:1-5
10. John 14:12

02: POWERFULLY CONVICTED MEN: MORALITY—SIMPLE BUT STRONG

1. Iris Carreras, "Christopher Lane, Australian Baseball Player, Killed by 'Bored' Teens, Police Say," *CBS News*, August 20, 2013, http://www.cbsnews.com/ws/christopher-lane-australian-baseball-player-killed-by-bored-okla-teens-police-say/.

2. Matthew 5:14-16
3. Hebrews 10:38-39
4. Acts 13:22
5. James 1:6-8
6. Matthew 22:35-40
7. John 14:21
8. John 8:29
9. Luke 6:31-32
10. Quoted in David Crabtree, "I Will Build My Church," *Preaching Today*, no. 231, accessed March 6, 2018, http://www.preachingtoday.com/sermons/sermons/2007/april/iwillbuildmychurch.html.
11. 1 Timothy 6:12
12. Luke 6:40

03: POWERFULLY CONNECTED MEN: COMMUNITY—THE SPIRIT OF THE RAPSCALLION

1. Matthew 19:14
2. Luke 18:17
3. Timothy Keller with Kathy Keller, *The Meaning of Marriage: Facing the Complexities of Commitment with the Wisdom of God* (New York: Riverhead Books, 2011), 145.
4. Romans 8:28-29
5. Proverbs 2:20, NASB
6. Proverbs 13:20, NASB
7. Mark 8:35, NLT
8. 1 John 1:5-7
9. Proverbs 28:13
10. James 5:16
11. 2 Corinthians 12:9
12. Psalm 101:6
13. Proverbs 27:17, NASB
14. Proverbs 18:24
15. Hebrews 10:23-25
16. 1 Corinthians 12:21
17. Psalm 133, NASB
18. Acts 13:1-3, NASB

04: POWERFULLY IMPACTED WOMEN: DIGNITY—THE ARSONIST AND THE FIREFIGHTERS

1. Judges 4:8
2. Judges 5:1-2

3. Philippians 2:1-4, MSG
4. Philippians 2:14-16, MSG
5. Genesis 2:18, 21-22, MSG

05: POWERFULLY AFFECTED CHILDREN: LEGACY—WORTH AND PEACE

1. "Poll: Most Men Aspire to Be Dads," *USA Today*, June 15, 2013, https://www.usatoday.com/story/news/nation/2013/06/15/poll-most-men-aspire-to-be-dads/2427123/.
2. Miranda Hitti, "How Many Men Become Fathers," *Web MD*, June 1, 2006, accessed February 26, 2018, https://www.webmd.com/men/news/20060601/how-many-men-become-fathers.
3. "Dad Stats," *National Responsible Fatherhood Clearinghouse*, US Dept. of Health and Human Services, accessed February 26, 2018, https://www.fatherhood.gov/content/dad-stats.
4. Gretchen Livingston and Kim Parker, "A Tale of Two Fathers," *Pew Research Center* (report), June 15, 2011, http://www.pewsocialtrends.org/2011/06/15/a-tale-of-two-fathers/.
5. "On Understanding Orphan Statistics" (white paper), Christian Alliance for Orphans, accessed January 29, 2018, https://cafo.org/wp-content/uploads/2015/06/Christian-Alliance-for-Orphans-_On-Understanding-Orphan-Statistics_.pdf.
6. Gus Lubin, "There Are 42 Million Prostitutes in the World, and Here's Where They Live," *Business Insider*, January 17, 2012, http://www.businessinsider.com/there-are-42-million-prostitutes-in-the-world-and-heres-where-they-live-2012-1.
7. Isaiah 5:7, NASB
8. Matthew 3:16-17
9. "Statistics," *The Fatherless Generation*, accessed January 11, 2018, https://thefatherlessgeneration.wordpress.com/statistics/.
10. John 3:16
11. Romans 8:14-17
12. 2 Corinthians 5:15
13. Matthew 23:4
14. Ephesians 1:3-6

06: POWERFULLY DELIVERED JUSTICE: RELEVANCY—BRILLIANCE AND BLACKNESS

1. Philippians 2:12-16
2. Matthew 12:35
3. Matthew 5:38-42

4. Luke 22:24-27, NLT
5. Acts 2:42-47, NLT
6. Matthew 11:28-30, NLT
7. Galatians 6:2
8. 2 Corinthians 7:5-7
9. Acts 4:32-35
10. Ephesians 6:18
11. Phillipians 4:6-7
12. Proverbs 2:6-9
13. Proverbs 27:9, NASB
14. Proverbs 25:11-12, MSG
15. Matthew 20:28

07: POWERFULLY OPPOSED MOVEMENT: FEROCITY—TREACHERY, POWER, AND ZEAL

1. Ephesians 6:10-13, NASB
2. Matthew 10:1, 7-8, 16
3. Luke 6:46
4. John 17:17
5. Matthew 5:8
6. Galatians 5:13-15
7. Martin Luther King Jr., *The Papers of Martin Luther King Jr., Volume V: Threshold of a New Decade, January 1959-December 1960* (Berkeley: University of California Press, 2005), 224.
8. Theodore Roosevelt, "Citizenship in a Republic," speech delivered at the Sorbonne, Paris, France, April 23, 1910, accessed February 28, 2018, http://www.theodore-roosevelt.com/trsorbonnespeech.html.
9. 1 Peter 4:12-16
10. "China," Open Doors USA, accessed January 12, 2018, https://www.opendoorsusa.org/christian-persecution/world-watch-list/china/.
11. 2 Corinthians 4:11
12. Hebrews 10:35-39
13. Matthew 28:18

08: POWERFULLY REMEMBERED MEN: VISIBILITY—THE SONG OF THE UNSUNG

1. Acts 4:32-37
2. Romans 12:6-8
3. 2 Thessalonians 2:16-17
4. Luke 22:19
5. 1 Thessalonians 5:9-11

6. Hebrews 3:13
7. Acts 9:26-28
8. Matthew 7:13-14
9. Mark 8:35
10. Acts 11:22-24
11. John 14:16-18
12. Ephesians 5:17-20
13. Acts 15:36-41
14. Hebrews 6:10

09: POWERFULLY IMPASSIONED MEN: FERVENCY—THE ARRIVAL OF REVIVAL

1. Chris Castaldo, "Why Did God Use Spurgeon?," Gospelcoalition.org, January 8, 2013, https://www.thegospelcoalition.org/article/why-did-god-use-spurgeon/.
2. Roberts Liardon, comp., *Frank Bartleman's Azusa Street: Firsthand Accounts of the Revival* (Shippensburg, PA.: Destiny Image, 2006), 13.
3. Castaldo, "Why Did God Use Spurgeon?"
4. Acts 2:42-47
5. Matthew 9:16-17
6. Acts 3:1-10
7. Acts 4:2
8. Acts 4:7-12
9. Acts 4:23-24
10. Acts 4:24-30
11. Acts 4:31-33

10: POWERFULLY CALLED FORWARD: BRAVERY—UNDERSTANDING THE TIMES

1. Hollie McKay, "Catholic Men's Conference in Crosshairs of Left-Wing Activists," *Fox News*, July 27, 2017, http://www.foxnews.com/us/2017/07/27/catholic-mens-conference-in-crosshairs-left-wing-activists.html.

THE NAVIGATORS® STORY

———— ◐ ————

T HANK YOU for picking up this NavPress book! I hope it has
been a blessing to you.

NavPress is a ministry of The Navigators. The Navigators began
in the 1930s when a young California lumberyard worker named
Dawson Trotman was impacted by basic discipleship principles and
felt called to teach those principles to others. He saw this mission as
an echo of 2 Timothy 2:2: "And the things you have heard me say in
the presence of many witnesses entrust to reliable people who will
also be qualified to teach others" (NIV).

In 1933, Trotman and his friends began discipling members of the
US Navy. By the end of World War II, thousands of men on ships
and bases around the world were learning the principles of spiritual
multiplication by the person-to-person teaching of God's Word.

After World War II, The Navigators expanded its ministry to include
college campuses; local churches; the Glen Eyrie Conference Center
and Eagle Lake Camps in Colorado Springs, Colorado; and neighborhood and citywide initiatives across the country and around the world.

Today, with more than 2,600 US staff members—and local ministries in more than 100 countries—The Navigators continue the process of making disciples who make more disciples, advancing the Kingdom of God in a world that desperately needs the hope and salvation of Jesus Christ and the encouragement to grow deeper in relationship with Him.

NAVPRESS was created in 1975 to advance the calling of The Navigators by bringing biblically rooted and culturally relevant products to people who want to know and love Christ more deeply. In January 2014, NavPress entered into an alliance with Tyndale House Publishers to strengthen and better position our rich content for the future. Through *The Message* Bible and other resources, NavPress seeks to bring positive spiritual movement to people's lives.

If you're interested in learning more or becoming involved with The Navigators, go to www.navigators.org. For more discipleship content from The Navigators and NavPress authors, visit www.thedisciplemaker.org. May God bless you in your walk with Him!

Sincerely,

DON PAPE
VP/PUBLISHER, NAVPRESS

www.navpress.com

CP1308